Get Over Yourself!

Get Over Yourself!

7 PRINCIPLES TO GET OVER YOUR PAST AND ON WITH YOUR PURPOSE

By Jennifer Beckham

DESTINY IMAGE® PUBLISHERS, INC.

P.O. Box 310, Shippensburg, PA 17257-0310

"Speaking to the Purposes of God for This Generation and for the Generations to Come."

This book and all other Destiny Image, Revival Press, MercyPlace, Fresh Bread, Destiny Image Fiction, and Treasure House books are available at Christian bookstores and distributors worldwide.

For a U.S. bookstore nearest you, call 1-800-722-6774.

For more information on foreign distributors, call 717-532-3040.

Reach us on the Internet: www.destinyimage.com

Typesetting Design: PerfecType, Nashville, TN, 2009

Cover Design: Tim Dahn, Inspire Digital Images, Jacksonville, FL, 2009

Trade Paper ISBN 13: 978-0-7684-3818-5
Hardcover ISBN: 978-0-7684-3819-2
Large Print ISBN: 978-0-7684-3820-8
E-book ISBN: 978-0-7684-8983-5

Printed in the United States of America

2 3 4 5 6 7 8 9 10 / 15 14 13 12 11

Dedication

This book is dedicated to...

The most amazing woman I will ever know:
my mom, Marie Mitchell! For your endless generosity
and love. You truly are my hero! I love you forever!

Anthony, the real Prince Charming! Thank you for your
life-changing love and your promise to follow me wherever I go.
I love you forever!

My gorgeous children, Cole and Jordan. You are the two
greatest contributions I will ever make to this world!
Mommy loves you so much!

And most importantly, my Lord, my Savior, my Deliverer,
Jesus Christ: for getting me over myself and on with my destiny!
I love You, Lord!

In loving memory of my dad, Darryl Mitchell (1938–1989):
for always encouraging me to convince myself.

Acknowledgments

My Savior and Lord: for setting me on this most difficult and wonderful journey. Thank You for the motivation and inspiration to show up and follow through. For Your grace, Your guidance, and Your enduring love. I am nothing without You.

My husband and best friend, Anthony, and my two incredible children, Cole and Jordan: for the countless hours you sacrificed keeping each other entertained so I could have time to write. You three are my most cherished gifts from God! I love you forever!

My amazing mom: for being the greatest mother, friend, and Meme a daughter could have. Thank you, Mom, for always loving me, supporting me, investing in me, and believing in me—no matter what! I love you so very, very much!

My family: to Mama with love. Shelley and Alex for all your enthusiasm and continued help with the kids. Todd and Shannon (and Brookie), for your trust and faithfulness to the call—WOW! (Thank God for that parking space!) I love you all!

All my love to (my brother) Kevin and Julia and Kayleigh...and to the countless other brave soldiers and their families serving our country, preserving our freedom. Thank you!

My outstanding (original) editor and friend, Amy Parker: Thank you for finding "me" and digging me out. For investing far more of yourself than you bargained for—thank you!!!

My "GAP" partners and friends: for your unbelievable support and love as WE—together—carry this message and extend His most amazing grace. Thank you for your encouragement, your prayers, and for sowing into this project! I love you all!

Tim Dahn: Thank you for bringing this book to life with your beautiful cover design! For your tireless patience with me and my perfectionism! (And for Maria's warm hospitality!) You are truly a Godsend! May God explode your business: www.InspireDigitalImages.com

Stephen Ginesi of SDG-Pictures: Thank you for allowing us to use your photo for our cover. You are a truly gifted photographer. May God bless you and your business!

Dan and Ang DePriest at Scribe Book Company: for all your hard work on my original (hardcover) edition. Thank you.

My friend Lesa Henderson: for helping me take the first big step of getting it all out and onto paper. I am so grateful to you! Love you, girl!

To my beloved friends in Alaska (you know who you are!): May this be the longest, most intelligent book you've ever read! Love you guys!

And to you, my friend: for taking the time and making the effort to get over yourself and on with your destiny. May the message of this book be as freeing for you as it is for me, and may your life be blessed and forever changed for having taken this journey with me!

Endorsements

"Jennifer Beckham knows firsthand that life isn't a fairy tale. While living out her dream as a Disney princess, she was miserable inside. She shares in these pages how she found fulfillment and healing—and provides valuable principles to help others achieve their God-given destiny."

JAMES & BETTY ROBISON
Co-Hosts, LIFE Today Television
Fort Worth, Texas

"Jennifer's God-given gift of communication along with her authentic devotion to help women overcome insecurities makes this book a "Life Changer". Her powerful testimony will equip and inspire you with life-giving truths from God's Word. She is walking in an anointing for such a time as this and she knows firsthand how to guide you through a healing journey of hope."

Jackie Garner
Director of Women's Ministry, Lakewood Church
Houston, TX
www.lakewood.cc

"Jennifer's journey is a real "rags to riches" story of a princess who didn't know she came from a royal bloodline! Her story is captivating, relevant, and so needful! It's time for the church to hit the real issues that religion and rules can't fix. Thank you Jennifer for being HIS voice!"

Sandi Krakowski

CEO, A Real Change Int'l

www.sandikrakowski.com

"Every little girl longs to be a princess and within every woman is that little girl. In her book, *Get Over Yourself*, Jennifer Beckham candidly shares how her little girl princess dreams turned into an all-too-grown-up nightmare. Weaving Biblical principles throughout, as well as practical, chapter-ending reflective portions, Jennifer tenderly leads us to stop grieving our lost fairy tale and begin embracing God's divine 'ever after'. Jennifer Beckham powerfully speaks into the hearts of women of all ages!"

Ann Mainse

Host, Full Circle TV Show

"I highly recommend this book to anyone who wants to move on with God and leave the mundane life of a "me" mentality. Jennifer has done an excellent job of taking seven principles based on the Word of God that, when applied, will take the reader to a fulfilling and exciting life with God!"

Jane D'Andrea

Co-host of "The Good Life"

and Wife of CTN President and Founder

Bob D'Andrea

"Jennifer's book challenged me to see God in a deeper way, as my deliverer. Her words enabled me to open my heart to God and trust Him enough to look at my hurts and heal them. From that place of healing God will be able to use me in an authentic way."

Denise Wylie
Light Line Host
WPOS-FM Radio
www.WPOSfm.com

"I'm a practical girl. That's why I love that Jennifer's book addresses specific things from our past and present that are keeping us from moving forward. She offers practical action steps to identify the issues and then how to heal and move past it so that you can 'Get Over Yourself' and on with your destiny!"

Janel Dinley
Founder of True Daughters
www.truedaughters.net

Contents

Life Is No Fairy Tale

*You may not realize it when it happens, but a
kick in the teeth may be
the best thing in the world for you.*
~ WALT DISNEY

"If Jesus forgave all my sins, why don't I feel any different?"

"If God loves me so much, why did He allow that to happen?"

"I am constantly haunted by my past. How do I let go?"

"I'm just so empty inside."

"There's no way God has a purpose for a person like me!"

*"If God has this great purpose for my life, why won't He show me
what it is?!"*

I could not even begin to log the number of hours that I have spent
around tear-stained altars hearing from women of all ages whose
dreams have been broken or cast aside by the pains and reality of
this life, women who are searching for purpose, passion, forgiveness, fulfillment, healing...*help.*

After more than a decade of being brought into the inner lives of women, hearing these common confessions and quests, I decided to put my responses on paper. This book is my answer—my mass response, if you will—to the countless women and young ladies who have come searching for answers to these pertinent issues that plague many of our lives.

I am not a counselor, or a psychologist, or even a world-renowned authority on…well, anything. I am a woman with issues, trials, and temptations—just like you—who is passionate about finding answers to these crippling questions. I am a woman who's been there—at the same altars, with the same lingering questions, concerns, and fears. Like you, I have experienced the joy of realizing some amazing dreams-come-true and have also experienced the pain and devastation of realizing that those dreams will not fulfill all the longings of a heart as they so often promise. And now, finally, I have been fortunate enough to find some answers that have literally changed my life.

> *I am a woman with issues, trials, and temptations—just like you.*

As far back as I can remember, I've always been a dreamer; I suppose that's why I loved Disney so much. Growing up in Florida, all of our family vacations were spent at Walt Disney World in Orlando.

My mom, my sister, and I especially loved the nighttime spectacle, "The Main Street Electrical Parade." It never mattered how exhausted we were from a day of adventure in the four lands that made up the Magic Kingdom; we always mustered the energy to stay late and enjoy that beautiful parade.

As I stood next to my mom, I watched in wonder as Cinderella's stagecoach glided past me. She was absolutely beautiful in her glittering gown, perched serenely in her carriage. I thought she was everything a princess should be. As I snapped her picture, she smiled and waved. Cinderella waved directly at *me*! In that moment, my seven-year-old heart raced with excitement, and I looked up at my mom with innocent confidence, "Mommy, I'm going to be a princess when I grow up!" Funny thing is, when I said it, I somehow knew I wasn't just dreaming. I *was* going to be a princess when I grew up—somewhere inside of me, I *knew* it!

My dream came true! I was chosen to be a Disney Princess.

Eleven years later, my dream came true! I was chosen to be a Disney Princess. Only, instead of waltzing straight to my magical destiny, I took an unexpected turn into a nightmare. I began to wander down a twisted road of harsh comparisons, fierce competition, and a continual demand for perfection. This in turn brought me into a secret life of depression and destructive behaviors. Not only repulsed by my appearance, I also hated who and what I'd become. I feared my dreams had been shattered forever.

It wasn't Disney's fault. It was my pursuit of the endless search for fulfillment that took me to the depths of despair and back. The best I can remember, "the chase" started in high school, just after my dad passed away with cancer. He had always been there to cheer me on to my next victory, and the Lord knows, it was always my goal to make him proud. But with my dad gone, I just kept running, kept chasing the next acknowledgment, the next trophy. When relationships no longer fulfilled me, I quickly moved on to the next. I chased it all as hard as I could, never stopping to acknowledge the thought that consumed my life: *If I could just get* there, then *I will be happy*."

> *If I could just get there, then I will be happy.*

Yet, if I had taken the time to absorb Psalm 16:11, I would have discovered: "You [*God*] will make known to me the path of life; in *Your presence* is fullness of joy; in *Your right hand* there are pleasures forever" (NASB, emphasis mine). Eventually, midway through my contracted time with Disney, I gave my broken heart and life over to God—my first step toward true happiness.

Elizabeth Barrett Browning once wrote, "God's gifts put man's best dreams to shame," and, boy, was she right! In the end, God taught me that He had a much bigger dream for my life than any I had conceived. After marrying a preacher within eight weeks of meeting him, I was launched into a life of ministry. I eventually came into my own personal relationship with God and was called to preach God's Word.

Before I could teach others, however, God required me to work through some major issues in my own life. I had to learn to overcome the fickle feelings that were hindering the development of my own faith. God actually put it this way to me: "It's time to *get over yourself!*" A bit harsh? Maybe. But what I came to understand was that *I* was the one standing in the way of God's plans for my life. He wanted me to get over my own *self* issues—my self-hatred, lack of confidence and self-esteem, my fears, feelings of rejection, and deep-seated anger—so I could begin to reach out to others. My personal issues were hindering my ability to just *believe*—believe that He loved me, that He called me, that I was chosen by Him to do great things on this earth, that He had a perfect plan for my life despite the hideous condition I was in when He found me.

As we worked through these issues, God, in a miraculous epiphany, taught me the principles I share in this book. I call them Princess Principles. He took me back to a moment in my former Disney days, and He correlated my present life as His princess with my former life as a Disney Princess. In doing so, He revealed earth-shattering truths that delivered me from mere feeling *for* God into a real faith *in* God. And, as a result, He ultimately delivered me from myself.

But these principles, I've discovered, aren't just for me. Now I know that God gave them to me to share with *you* too, as a roadmap out of our "self issues" and into a life free from shame, guilt, regret, anger, and insecurity.

If you're searching, hurting, mourning, yearning, or just scratching your head at your lack of contentment, these principles will give you practical answers to the questions on your mind, no matter what your age or stage in life. If you strive to develop your faith and get over your own self issues—issues that interfere with your ability to believe in *your*self and in the sovereignty of *your* Creator—then this book is for you. It will shape godly character in you that is essential for living a consistent, faith-filled life. It will help you to cleverly confront real-life issues, while also leading you to discover your true worth. And it will give you the confidence to be your best each and every day, one day at a time.

> *"It's time to get over yourself!"*

So, if you're ready for a life-changing fairy tale, step into the carriage with me. But be warned: Our travels will take us to an imperfect world, with an imperfect princess, on a fumbling, grueling attempt to find her true destiny.

But as with all fairy tales, she *will* find it.

And so can you.

CHAPTER 1

Once Upon a Time

*"For I know the plans I have for you," declares
the Lord, "plans to prosper you and not to harm
you, plans to give you hope and a future."*
~ JEREMIAH 29:11

It was one of my worst mornings yet—the morning after my family had flown back to the States. When they arrived, it was the first time I had seen a face from home in the three months I had been working for Tokyo Disneyland. But when they left, their departure had only magnified my loneliness.

We had spent ten wonderful days touring the country, exploring the beautiful landscapes, eating local cuisine, laughing, talking, and crying. It was an amazing time to share together.

The only thing that could have made our visit more perfect was snow. Born and raised in Florida, I had never experienced the joy of winter's first snowfall. While in Tokyo, though, I *knew* it would snow, and I had been anticipating it all season. Since it hadn't come yet, I just knew I'd experience my first snow with my family there. But it didn't happen.

Then, about an hour after my family left for the airport, little white flakes started trickling down from the clouds. We had missed it. And with every flake that fell, my heart sank even lower. I was thousands of miles away from home, with five months still left of my eight-month entertainer's contract, and desperately in need of the love only a family can give.

I lay in bed that night sobbing into my pillow and missing my family so badly I could hardly stand it. I felt completely alone, and knowing that I had to spend five *more* months away from them was unbearable. I really wanted to die.

In an attempt to bury my pain, I did what any good bulimic would do. I walked into the kitchen and began devouring everything in it. If it wasn't nailed down, I ate it. I shoved everything and anything I could find in my mouth. After I had scarfed down my entire stash of goodies, I went after my roommate's stash too. I wasn't too concerned about her finding out; I had become really good at rearranging food to make it look like it hadn't been touched.

The binge was followed by the inevitable purge. I knew that I had to get rid of all I had consumed to fit into my costume the next day, so I spent the remainder of the night throwing up. Skillfully pushing my fingers deep into my throat, I made myself vomit until I felt like my heart was going to rip through my chest with the next violent purge.

The next morning, I pried myself up from the cold, hard bathroom floor where I had fallen asleep after exhausting myself from the seemingly endless cycle of binging and purging. Needless to say, I was not feeling well. And the last thing in the world I wanted to do was get up and go be Cinderella.

I desperately wanted to call in sick. Unfortunately, that wasn't an option. I had just taken several days off to spend time with my family. I had no choice but to go into work.

After much internal debate, I somehow found the will and energy to haul myself off of the floor and into my clothes. I did not, however, have the strength to shower—a detail that most certainly *should* have been considered a necessity at this point. But getting up, dressed, and to my shuttle bus on time was all I could manage. I dragged my depressed, withered self into work…to be, of all things, a *princess*.

As I entered the building backstage, Tommy was there to greet me as usual. Tommy was the supervisor and liaison for our cast. He was our translator, our boss, and the main link between the American and Japanese coworkers. He was Asian, but where sarcasm, speech, and attitude were concerned, Tommy was as American as we were.

The last thing I wanted to do was get up and go be Cinderella.

He oversaw every event and show, but his biggest responsibility was to keep all sixteen of the American entertainers happy and working peacefully with the Japanese staff and crew members who made our jobs possible. To me, Tommy was more like our shadow. He involved himself in every aspect of our lives, on the stage and off. His sharp eye missed few details, and as I entered the greenroom, he looked inquisitively at me. "What's wrong with you?" he asked.

I was doing well just to be there and was certainly not in the mood for his snide remarks, so I answered quickly, "Nothing, Tommy, I'm fine."

But Tommy didn't buy it. And he didn't let it go. "You don't look so good. Are you sick?"

"No. I'm fine," I lied. "Just let me get my makeup on, and I'll be fine." I walked with my head down as I was going by him, hoping he wouldn't see just how right he was. Even I had begun noticing that my skin and teeth were turning a strange gray color. Plus, my body was bloated—not exactly the result you're looking for when trying to squeeze into a tiny costume.

However, Tommy reached out and grabbed my arm, spinning me toward him. "No, you're not fine," he insisted. "Now tell me what's wrong with you." He continued gripping my arm so that I couldn't turn away from him.

In that moment, every unstable emotion I was feeling came charging to my lips; and before I realized what I was doing, I lifted my head, looked him square in the eyes, and snapped, "Look, Tommy, I don't feel good, and I don't want to be here today, okay?! I just don't feel like doing this...I don't *feel* like a princess today, Tommy!"

The look in Tommy's eyes sent reality barreling into me like a train. I had just unloaded on my boss!

Hanging my head, I wiped the stream of tears that began slipping from my bloodshot eyes and waited. I halfway expected to receive some act of sympathy from Tommy—a hand on my shoulder, words of reassurance that everything was going to be all right, or even better, an "It's okay, honey, you go on home." After all, it was clear I had no business being there. I just wanted to go home, crawl in the bed, pull the covers over my head, and hide—and not just back to my apartment, but *home* to my family in the States.

After what seemed to be an eternity under Tommy's impenetrable gaze, he finally cleared his throat and spoke:

"Who ever asked you to feel?
You were chosen to be a princess.
Now go, wash your face, get a new attitude, put
on your clothes, and go be Cinderella!"

Although it sounded a lot like an angry boss reprimanding a slacking employee, Tommy had just delivered to me instructions of great biblical relevance. Of course, neither of us realized it at the time, but what I viewed then as a harsh and merciless reply turned out to be just the advice I needed to turn my life around. It would be years before I fully understood the depth of the instructions that Tommy had given to me that day.

It would be years before I understood the depth of the instructions.

Long after those fateful words were delivered to me, I discovered that these same instructions were delivered to biblical men and women of God. Maybe you've heard of them: David, Esther, Ruth, and Aaron. God was using Tommy's words and my Disney experience to illuminate and bring to life these biblical examples and to make a life-changing impact in my role as a believer. Maybe you'll find comfort, as I did, in knowing that even with these godly examples, each had similar internal struggles to just show up and fulfill each of their God-given purposes. Unbeknownst to Tommy, he was the person sent to instruct me and point me toward my purpose, and perhaps I am sent to you to instruct you and point you to yours.

Tommy's words, "Who ever asked you to feel? You were *chosen* to be a princess. Now go, wash your face, get a new attitude, put on your clothes, and go be Cinderella!" contain promise and specific biblical directions toward our God-given destiny.

In the Bible, of course, Aaron wasn't called to play the role of princess but was called and anointed to be Israel's very first high priest. However, he first had to deal with the guilt of his sin—leading people away from God by permitting and aiding them in the worship of other gods. (See Exodus 29:1–7 and Exodus 32.)

God had big plans for them, if they could only conquer the weakness of self.

David was called to be king of Israel over God's chosen people, but he first had to deal with the very knowledge that he failed God and fell short of what he was called to be: God's chosen king. (See 2 Samuel 11–12.)

Esther was called to deliver all of God's people, the Jews, from a holocaust under the hands of Haman. But first she had to deal with the loss of her parents and being taken from the only family she had, her cousin Mordecai, and gain confidence in a strange place, King Xerxes' palace. (See the book of Esther.)

Ruth was called to be a part of the very lineage of Jesus Christ through a second marriage, but first she had to deal with the grief of her first husband's death and all the changes that came with it. (See the book of Ruth.)

Each of these men and women of God were called by God to accomplish great things, yet they faced setbacks and tragedy that required them to *get over themselves* before moving forward. For Aaron and David, their poor choices—their sins—were the very causes of their own setbacks. Aaron had led God's people into idol worship, and King David committed adultery and then had the woman's husband murdered. Theirs were not minor offenses. But God had big plans for them, if they could only conquer the weakness of self and come to rely on Him.

Esther and Ruth were met with circumstances over which they had no control. They had both lost loved ones. Esther's parents and

Ruth's husband had died. Both women had to deal with the grief of those losses and then with the uncertainty of moving from their homes to a foreign place with unfamiliar surroundings. But God must have known that overcoming these tragedies would build the strength of character needed to fulfill the purposes He had in store for them.

And then there's me: a lonely, bulimic "princess" in a strange place, still searching for the lost love of a father and the guidance of her Heavenly Father. Had I possessed the knowledge or faith at that time to compare myself to these great biblical figures, perhaps my outlook would have been much different. But I didn't. And it wasn't.

What about you? Are you facing setbacks and tragedies of your own variety? Are they products of your own poor choices, or are you a victim of circumstance? Maybe it happened years ago, and you never really dealt with it completely. Maybe it's happening now, and your outlook is just as mine was: bleak, hopeless, and with little understanding of God's ultimate plan.

That's okay. You're in great company. Once upon a time, Aaron, David, Esther, Ruth...and even *I* walked this same uncertain path. Whether you're walking it now or should've dealt with the issue by walking this path ten years ago, let's keep going and face the dragons of your fairy tale together. As we

Let's face the dragons of your fairy tale together.

continue, we'll learn more about the paths we'll need to take and the weapons we'll need to carry to make it through. Never fear— once we make it to the other side, we'll find God's purpose there waiting for us.

Who ever asked you to feel?

You were chosen to be a princess!

Now go...

Wash your face...

Get a new attitude...

Put on your clothes...

And go be Cinderella!

CHAPTER 2

"Who Ever Asked You to Feel?"

PRINCESS PRINCIPLE #1:
CHOOSE TO ACT ON FAITH, NOT FEELINGS.

We live by faith, not by sight.
~ 2 CORINTHIANS 5:7

Although I was shocked and wounded by Tommy's words, the message that became immediately clear to me was that my job called for me to perform my role *regardless* of how I felt at the time. I was hired to play the characters of happy, perfect little girls whose countenance simply glowed with a passion for life. These singing, smiling, dancing, skipping characters were quite opposite from a depressed, miserable bulimic who was sticking her finger down her throat and wishing for death. The position I was chosen to fill there at Disney was far different from the way I had come to feel. But even though my emotions had left me feeling quite ill equipped for the job at hand, I was still expected to get beyond my fickle feelings and do what I was chosen to do. And I believe the same is true for us today.

"FEELINGS, OH-WO-WO FEELINGS!"

My need to "feel" things began at an early age. My siblings would be the first to tell you that out of all of us, I was by far the most emotionally sensitive and severely high-maintenance child when it came to attention. At a very young age, I began leaving long letters on the counter at night addressed to my parents. These letters looked for love, attention, or sympathy for how my brothers and sister had treated me that day. Then somewhere around sixth grade, I began having major difficulties with girls—dealing with all the meanness, jealousies, bullying, backbiting, rumors, and the constant emotional drama that often comes with being a teenage girl. The mistreatment became so brutal after the death of my father in my freshman year of high school that I had sworn off female friendships altogether. Unfortunately, in the absence of good girlfriends to see me through that difficult time, I began looking for love and acceptance in the arms of boys—one unhealthy relationship after another. I was always searching for that something or someone who could give me the feeling I was longing for.

I thought I'd finally found it when Disney hired me. Being chosen by Disney was the ultimate affirmation for me, a dream come true that I knew would fill my life with the worthiness and belonging I had so long been searching for. I believed that if I could just get up on top of that princess float, then I would feel so much better about myself.

Of course, I was again mistaken.

There was, however, one aspect of my plan that was accurate. I *would* find the answer I had been searching for while working for Disney in Tokyo. But it was in a place I had never expected—in the arms of a man named Jesus.

One night, after work, two castmates nearly dragged me to a Billy Graham Crusade at the Tokyo Dome. I wouldn't have even gone except that I knew that if I stayed home, I would spend the first half of the night gorging myself with food and the rest of it hugging the toilet. That was the night I was introduced to a caring God who, I learned, loved me so much that He sent His Son, Jesus, to die for my failures and sins. I discovered that night that God knew everything about me—every last gory detail about my shameful past. Yet, He said that He loved me anyway, the way no other man ever could. He offered me the unconditional love and acceptance that I had so desperately longed for. I believed Him and vowed my broken heart to Him that night.

Jesus and I hung out together, and for a while it was everything I'd hoped our relationship would be. I needed Him to be there for me, and I wanted to be free of the pain of my past. I talked to Him. I told Him my secrets, my fears, and my disappointments. I told Him that I needed His help to feel differently about myself. I thought that maybe *this* relationship would be the one to last.

I really wanted to be different, but as much as my life needed to be different at that point, I wasn't really willing to work that hard to make changes. I never got involved in a Bible-believing church, I failed to spend any time getting to know more about how to grow my newfound faith,

> I wanted to be different, but I wasn't willing to change.

and I didn't put any personal effort toward trying to understand the Bible that I was given to read. If I had, I might have read His promise that *He would never leave or forsake me,* whether I *felt* Him or not.

I suppose, at the time, I was looking to God almost as any other man in my life—someone who would meet my needs and give me a quick fix for my emptiness. After a while, the passion, the strong feeling I'd first had when I accepted Him into my life, began to fade. Because I didn't *feel* Him with me, I stopped calling on Him. And, like all my past relationships, we started to grow apart, and I fell back into searching for love in all the wrong places.

I know now that Jesus remained there in my heart, loving me regardless of my feelings for Him. But that was too much for me to grasp at the time. I was so busy clinging to my own self, my own issues, at the time that I couldn't fully embrace all He had to offer. Thankfully, years later, my endless chase for the next emotional high led me to utter exhaustion and eventually brought me straight back into the arms of God once more.

When I finally found my way back to the Lord and started really putting forth an effort in building my faith and my relationship with God by praying, seeking after God's will for my life, and attending church, I remember just how confusing it all was at times. Always hearing people use a lot of "feeling" words to describe God and their experiences with Him, I got the impression that *everyone's* faith was tied to their feelings.

I would hear people in church say that they could *feel* the presence of God, *feel* His love, or *see* His hand upon their lives. I would listen to people talk about how they *heard* from God about something they had been praying about. I heard my pastor say that we should reach up and "touch the Lord," and another time he said that we should "taste and see" that the Lord is good. (I know now that he was referring to a verse in Scripture from Psalm 34:8).

One thing that was particularly confusing to me was that the very same people who were "feeling God" in miraculous ways one week were also the ones who were struggling in their faith the next because they weren't "feeling" Him as they thought they should. I'd already been there once before, after just giving my heart to the Lord in Japan, and I truly didn't want to be like them—a "roller-coaster Christian," up one day and down the next, following after my fickle feelings. I recognized the need to ground my faith in something more stable. But it surely wasn't easy, and I didn't know how.

I will never forget the moment that God first revealed to me that despite my best efforts, I had become just like those I'd witnessed in church—a shallow, roller-coaster Christian. It's not exactly the message you hope to have spoken into your spirit. Yet, at the time, I was desperately frustrated that I could not feel God like I wanted to. There had been so many times in my life that I could *feel* His awesome presence as others had described. It was especially strong in the first year or so of my relationship with Him. Then, after a little while of getting to know God more intimately, there was a period of months that His presence seemed so far off, like He had left me.

After months of being aggravated and frustrated toward God for His unwillingness to just "show up" as I was asking of Him, He finally answered me. One morning, as I was getting out of bed, I recall having the conversation with myself. (I had stopped talking to God since I assumed He wasn't listening anyway.) I thought, *Maybe what I had with God wasn't really real. Maybe it was just a phase...*

Then out of the blue, I had a thought pass through my mind; it was most definitely a word from God into my spirit. He said, *You have feelings for Me, but not a true faith in Me.*

It stopped me dead in my tracks, and I began to examine those words. He was right: I was completely caught up in feelings and emotions toward and for God. As long as He was there, making my skin tingle or the hair stand up on the back of my neck, I stood firm in what I thought was faith. And as soon as the feelings stopped, I began to question my faith, my relationship with God.

But that wasn't true faith at all. Faith is all about *believing*, not feeling. And belief is a decision, a daily choice that we make about whom and what to trust—as an act of our free will. Through His wisdom and guidance, I have come to discover the truth: This is a *faith* walk, not a feeling walk.

> ***...we live by believing and not by seeing.***
> ~ 2 Corinthians 5:7 NLT

GETTING OFF THE ROLLER COASTER

So how do we keep from doing just that? How do we—as women, hard-wired emotionally by God Himself—keep from living our lives from emotion to emotion? How do we ground our faith on something more stable? How do we walk by faith anyway? First of all, let me start out by assuring you that if you are one who tends to "roller-coaster" your way through your life—or more importantly, your spiritual life—as I once have, it may be helpful for you to know that we are not alone.

It is okay to have emotions, as long as emotions don't have you!

And secondly, it's important to note here that God is the author of emotions. He created them and instilled them in us—and for good reason. Through emotion, we experience life—the good, the bad, and the necessary. Without emotion, we would never feel the joy of a newborn child or the signals of fear when we're in danger. Emotions serve an integral purpose in our lives, yet, as with anything, they can get out of control if left unchecked. And that's why this teaching is so vitally important. You must understand that it is okay to have emotions, as long as emotions don't have you!

Faith vs. Fear

According to Dr. Caroline Leaf, every emotion results in an attitude—an attitude of faith or an attitude of fear.[1] That is because there are only two types of emotion: faith-based and fear-based. She explains, "Examples of faith-based emotions are love, joy, peace, happiness, kindness, self-control, forgiveness, and patience. These produce good attitudes." She adds, "Examples of fear-based emotions are hate, worry, anxiety, anger, hostility, rage, ill-will, resentment, frustration, impatience, and irritation."

Fear is the opposite of faith, and we have the ability to choose which we will walk in. You can easily see how walking around with fear-based emotions could produce negative attitudes and belief systems that ultimately lead to negative behaviors. For example, if I walk around feeling frustrated and impatient all the time, it is going to affect my relationships negatively. If I walk around worried and anxious, I obviously do not trust God and His provision for my life; I'm operating in fear, being led by my feelings instead of my faith in God.

By the same token, if I walk around with faith-based emotions, my attitude and my behavior are going to be more positive. If I feel joyful and at peace, believing that I am loved and accepted, choosing to follow God and trust Him at His Word, then my relationships will be better, and I will be fulfilled in everything I put my hand to. If I choose to control my emotions, if I allow God to help me forgive others of their daily offenses, I am choosing to do life God's way. As a result, I will be at peace and happy in life.

Emotions are thoughts put into motion.

Emotions are essentially thoughts put into motion—we just have to decide where they'll take us. The problem arises when we do not keep our emotions in check and ground them on the Truth of God's Word instead of what our five senses are telling us to do. You see, awareness and control of our emotions keep them serving us—not the other way around.

Feelings and desires are powerful forces. Desire is the fuel that will drive us to our destiny, but again, we must choose the destination. Desire can drive an athlete like Michael Phelps to win fourteen Olympic gold medals or a dictator like Adolph Hitler to execute more than six million European Jews.

THE DEVIL MADE ME DO IT!

We've all heard, "The devil made me do it!" Well, of course, the devil can't really *make* you and me do anything, but he sure does try to help us along in our decision-making process. He plays on our feelings and desires to get to our free will, just as he did with Eve in the Garden of Eden. He led her to choose to disobey God's instruction. And how did he do it? The same way he still does it today: by enticing us through our feelings, specifically our five senses.

Let's look at how it all went down.

In Genesis 2 we see that God had taken the man, Adam, placed him in the Garden of Eden, and gave him permission to eat of any of the trees in the garden except for just one—the Tree of the Knowledge of Good and Evil. God said to Adam, "You must not eat from the tree…, for when you eat of it *you will surely die*" (v. 17, emphasis mine). God told Adam he would "surely die"—maybe not physically, but certainly spiritually by being separated from the presence of God.

Then in Genesis 3:4 the serpent, or the enemy, came along and challenged Eve on God's command. He ultimately fed her a lie, saying, "You will not surely die." The enemy's words were the polar opposite of God's. However, we know that God's words were true because God cannot lie (see Titus 1:2; Heb. 6:18).

God spoke the Truth. The enemy spoke a lie. And there Eve stood—where we've been standing ever since—between the Truth and the lie with her own free will to choose.

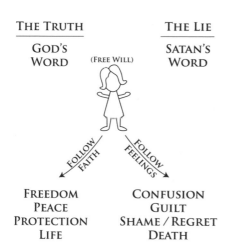

THE TRUTH

GOD'S WORD (FREE WILL)

FREEDOM
PEACE
PROTECTION
LIFE

THE LIE

SATAN'S WORD

CONFUSION
GUILT
SHAME / REGRET
DEATH

To follow after faith would mean she chooses to believe and trust God and His word, regardless of emotions. To follow after feelings, in this particular case, would mean that Eve would choose to trust the enemy, who had targeted her emotions, and *his* word. So what did the woman choose? She chose to follow after her feelings.

We see some evidence of this in Genesis 3:6–7. And note all of the words dealing with the senses: "When the woman *saw* that the fruit of the tree was good for food and *pleasing to the eye*, and also *desirable* for gaining wisdom, she took some and *ate* it. She also gave some to her husband, who was with her, and he *ate* it. Then the *eyes* of both of them were opened, and they *realized* they were *naked*; so they sewed fig leaves together and made coverings for themselves" (emphasis mine).

It's interesting to note that the word *opened* in verse 7 is translated from the Hebrew word *pa^qach*, which means "to open (the senses, especially the eyes)...to be observant."[2] When gaining "the knowledge of good *and* evil," their senses were awakened, causing them to observe another way of living—a way apart from God's way.

Until that very moment, God's way had been the only way. God's voice had been the only "voice" they had listened and responded to. Up to that point, they had lived life with an unfailing, childlike faith in their Father, God—with no thought of doing otherwise. They had never been introduced to the prospect of doing life their own way, independent from God and apart from His will. When given the choice, Adam and Eve chose their way, their will. They chose to follow after a life based on feeling rather than faith.

And God knew it—He knew that another, opposing "voice" had entered into their lives and introduced them to another way of thinking. We see proof of that when God showed up in the garden and asked Adam, "Who told you that you were naked?" (Gen. 3:11). In other words, "Who told you that you were in need of something other than what I could give you? Who told you that there was another way besides Mine?"

I particularly love this question that God challenged Adam with, "Who told you that you were naked?" because it is within this one question that God also gives us insight into how you and I can determine who—and what—to listen to: We need only to consider the source!

God was asking Adam to consider the source—"Who told you...?" and as I often like to add: "What convinced you...?" And I believe that God is showing us, too, that there are opposing "voices" constantly vying for our attention, standing in opposition to His Truth, and attempting to woo us emotionally into agreement with their lies. There, in the garden, it was the literal voice of the enemy speaking to Eve, but for us today, it may be the "voice" of someone, something, or even life experience that "speaks" to us and gets us all tangled up emotionally until we become convinced of the enemy's lies.

You see, satan, conniving as he is, knew he could not force Eve to eat of the fruit, so did the next best thing—he led her by her feelings (her "five senses"). Eve made her own choice to go against God's will for her life. Satan used the external world to get to Eve's internal thoughts. He knew that if he could stimulate her senses, move her emotionally, in order to affect her free will, she would ultimately choose for herself to go with her will and against God's will for her life, further leading to a life of guilt and shame. Satan went straight for her "feeler," her soul. And he uses that same tactic on us today.

HE SAVED MY...SOUL?

Psalm 143:3 says that satan is the enemy of our soul. But Psalm 23:3 says that God is the restorer of our souls. In order to best understand the importance of those verses, we might want to break down exactly what the soul is comprised of. After all, if satan is the enemy of our souls, it might be helpful to see what he's after so we can defend our territory. And if we're going to dissect the soul, we may want to back up a bit to better understand that we, as human beings, are actually made up of three distinct parts: spirit, soul, and body (see 1 Thess. 5:23). A good way to explain this is that we are a spirit who has a soul that lives in a body. It's important to also understand that at the moment of our salvation experience, our spirit is changed or reborn (or "born again" as we often call it), but our soul must then be renewed by the Word of God (see Rom. 12:2) and our body and its incessant desires must be kept under subjection at all times (see 1 Cor. 9:27). Perhaps that's why we don't always "feel" saved—because how we think, how we feel and what we want doesn't automatically change just because we get "born again." Grasping this teaching will help us to better understand how the enemy weasels his way into our lives and moves us from faith into feelings, away from God's will. And as a result, we'll be better prepared to prevent it.

The Spirit

Our spirit, or what the apostle Paul calls "the inward man" (2 Cor. 4:16 KJV), is the part of us that God speaks to. It is the part of us that we must strengthen and build up daily in order for us to be strong in the Lord. It's *our* responsibility to strengthen our spiritual selves—nobody else's. Our spirit is the part of us that we make stronger by exercising and by feeding it. Prayer, or simply communicating with God, is excellent exercise. And the spirit's food of choice? The Word of God. Without prayer and the Word, we are left spiritually weak, much too weak to wage war against the enemy. But *with* them, we will be strong enough to choose what is right even when it doesn't *feel* good to our flesh.

> *It's our responsibility to strengthen our spiritual selves.*

Psalm 119:11 tells us that we are to hide the Word of God in our hearts so that we might not sin against God. Feeding your spirit with the Word of God will make you strong and healthy, changing you from the inside out. Now I'm not sure exactly *how* the Word strengthens us on the inside, but then again, I can't exactly tell you how eating a pound of warm, freshly baked chocolate chip cookies every day of our lives will make our thighs fatter either. I just know it does! (More on changing ourselves from the inside out in chapter 6.)

The Soul

While our spirit contacts the spiritual realm, the soul is what we use to contact the intellectual realm. It is comprised of five parts: the will, emotions, intellect, imagination, and memory. The goal of the enemy is to get to our will—just as he did with Eve in the garden. He may use the other four parts—emotions, intellect, imagination, and memory—to get to our will, but free will is the part of our brain that does our choosing, and it is the enemy's main target in the fight for our soul.

According to Dr. Caroline Leaf in her compelling book, *Who Switched Off My Brain?*[3] scientists believe that they have identified a genetic code for free will. She shows us that the only way the enemy

has access to our brains, or more specifically, to the free will part of our brain where we make choices, is through our five senses.

> **The way you think determines the way you feel,
> and the way you feel influences the way you act.**
> ~ Rick Warren[4]

Our five senses—what we see, hear, smell, taste, and touch—are the gateways to our minds, the contact point between our external and our internal worlds. That's why it is so important to be very careful what you watch, listen to, come in contact with, and choose to partake in. Make no mistake about it: External influences can become loud, opposing "voices" that can drown out the voice of God in our lives! Some of those external influences the enemy uses to affect our internal thoughts and emotions are books, magazines, television, movies, friends, music, and even sentimental keepsakes.

Let's take diet as an example. For three weeks now, you've been eating well, working out—you've lost eight pounds! Then comes that Dairy Queen commercial on TV, and soon you're craving a Blizzard! Commercial after enticing commercial, you begin to rationalize. You've been doing well...It sure would be a nice treat ...You can exercise it off...Before you know it, you're in the car, on your way to Dairy Queen. Then, no sooner than you've finished your Blizzard, you become overwhelmed with feelings of guilt and disgust for having caved in to the temptation. You wake up feeling lousy about yourself and your lack of willpower. And it was all because of a freewill decision that resulted from the awakening of your senses: what you saw, what you imagined it would taste like, and even the memory of how delicious your last Blizzard was. That's all it took. And *that* was an easy one.

How about a high school girl named Ashley who has just broken up with her boyfriend? She believed he was "the one" (even though statistics say that 92 percent of the time our high school sweethearts will not be our mates for life[5]). But the guy turned out to be an absolute sleaze-ball, who broke her heart and left her with a bad reputation.

So she's sitting on her bed late one night, doing fairly well with the breakup. Her friends continually remind her how he wasn't good for her, that she's better off without him. She's

> The enemy has access to our brains through our five senses.

doing her best to remind herself how much of a jerk he was, even though her heart is still longing to be with him. But then, "their song" comes on the radio, and she's instantly in tears. "How can I ever live without him?" she pines.

Lying back on the bed, she begins to cry as she reminisces about all their good times and just how special their love was for one another. And when "their song" ends, it's followed by another that brings back more memories of their time together. She slides off of her bed and walks to the closet, taking out a box marked "Bobby." Opening the box, she begins pulling out the photos of them from the beach and the movie ticket stubs she had saved from their dates. She picks up the wilted rose that he left on her car after baseball practice one day and smells it as if it still had a scent to it. Tears are streaming down her face now, and she glances over to the phone. "Maybe he still loves me," she says out loud. "Maybe we can still work it out…" She leans over toward the phone on her nightstand, picks it up, and dials his number. And the cycle of pain continues.

So what did her senses have to do with her freewill choice? Absolutely everything. Ashley could have chosen to shut off her radio, throw away those old photos, and pick up the phone to call a friend to remind her of what she already knew deep down inside— that she was better off without him. Those choices would have helped her regain proper perspective so she could make the next right choice. Instead, she chose to wallow in her pain, allowing the enemy to arouse her senses, her memory, her imagination, her intellect, her reasoning, and especially her emotions to get to her will. She ultimately made the choice; the enemy just helped her along in her decision making.

As illustrated in the diagram, the enemy's one goal is to get to your free will—period! In order to get to your will, he uses your outside environment to produce a thought. Thoughts then trigger your senses, which then trigger internal emotions, reasonings,

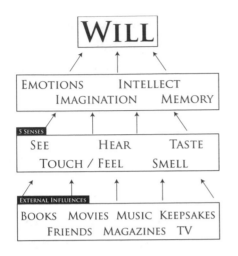

imaginations, or memories that lead us to act. And as long as the enemy can preoccupy us with thoughts, emotions, reasonings, vain imaginations, and memories, then we are spending all of our days wrestling with him instead of working for and walking with God.

Remember: Thoughts produce emotions...emotions lead us to act...acts become habits...habits become lifestyles...lifestyles forge character...character determines destiny.

The Body

The body is the third part of our being, and it is what we use to contact the physical realm. Like the soul, it is our responsibility to take command and to keep it in check. The body doesn't think; it just wants and craves. That's all.

It does speak, though, doesn't it? It certainly has a way of telling us what it wants and doesn't easily take no for an answer. It is relentless in its pursuit for more, more, more. The body and its cravings, when uncontrolled, will lead to a spiritual death. But Colossians 3:5 describes the control necessary to keep fleshly desires in check: "killing off everything connected with that way of death: sexual promiscuity, impurity, lust, doing whatever you feel like whenever you feel like it, and grabbing whatever attracts your fancy. That's a life shaped by things and feelings instead of by God" (MSG).

Did you hear that? God said to *kill it*. He didn't say to "try to avoid it" or "do your best to control it." He said to *kill* it! That's extreme! And how do you kill a desire? You starve it. If you choose not to feed that fleshly desire, eventually it will die.

In other words, if it's something that entices your flesh or arouses your senses to the point of being unable to control it, then get it out of your life and stop being led by your senses. God tells us in First Corinthians 9:27 that we are to keep our bodies under subjection at all times. God does not want you to live by feelings; we are called to live by faith in God's Word and instruction. Satan is the only one who ever asks you to feel.

The Ultimate Battle for Our Will

You see, what was compromised in the Garden of Eden that day was the ability to override our senses, to choose against the enemy's will, and to come into agreement with God's will. That day, Adam and Eve sacrificed the willpower of all mankind because they fell prey to following their feelings and disobeyed God's Word. Their perspective was changed when their eyes were opened, the five senses that governed their flesh were awakened, and they chose to disobey God to do it their own way.

Adam may have given up his willpower in the Garden of Eden, but we see another battle of wills in another garden, the Garden of Gethsemane. It was the first place where Jesus shed His blood for us on His way to the cross. He did it to redeem back our willpower from the enemy and to show us how it's done.

In the Gospel of Luke, we see Jesus going to the Garden of Gethsemane to pray and to plead with God to deliver Him from the coming events of His crucifixion. We see that Jesus was in so much agony and His soul was so exceedingly sorrowful that He was actually sweating drops of blood (see Luke 22:44). Then in Matthew, He cried out to God, His Father, "Let this cup pass from Me" (Matt. 26:39 NASB). In other words, "Lord, get Me out of this... Deliver Me from having to go through this period of death." Jesus made it clear that He did not *feel* like going to the cross. Then the strength of His spirit rose up within Him, and in the same verse, He concluded His prayer conceding to the will of God by adding, "yet not as I will but as You will." He knew what lay ahead. He knew death was certain if He continued in God's perfect will. And still He persisted in His faith. Jesus was the ultimate example of faith over feelings.

Just imagine where the world would be today had He decided to act on feelings and forego the pain of the cross.

GUIDANCE FROM YOUR FATHER

The God who created us knows far better than anyone—including ourselves—what is best for our lives. Following fleshly feelings will only lead us to go against God's instruction for our lives, inevitably leading us to destruction. But continually choosing to follow after faith instead of feelings will lead to a full, God-purposed life.

Through my ministry, I've heard a lot of teenagers and young adults saying that they feel like the Bible is a bunch of rules and laws and that God just wants to spoil all their fun and control their lives. And to that I'll share the best answer God has ever given me to that complaint. God is our Heavenly Father who, like any good parent, cares what comes of our lives. In so doing, He sets boundaries for us to live our lives in, and He does this for several reasons:

(1) to protect us from harm; (2) to preserve our lives; and (3) to provide something better for us.

As a parent myself, I understand all too well how children can push those boundaries. A few years ago, my children's friend stopped by one afternoon to ask if my kids—Cole, then age five, and Jordan, two—could play in the front yard of her house across the street. Jaclyn was about eight years old, and her mother was in the front yard with her, so I said yes. As they were heading out the door, I reminded Cole and Jordan that they were not allowed to play in the street.

Just moments later, while sitting at my desk in the upstairs office, I glanced out the front window to see Cole, Jordan, and Jaclyn playing in the street! In a flash, I was up and out of my chair, flying down the stairs toward the front door. Upon reaching the front door, I could see through the glass that my son was heading straight toward me. As we met in the foyer, Cole asked, huffing and puffing, "Mommy, is it okay that we play in the street?"

Something inside of Cole's gut told him he was snagged; hence, his question. Just then, I looked down at Cole, realizing that we had reached a crossroads in our relationship. I asked him, *"Who told you it was okay to play in the street?"* (Sound familiar?!)

You see, just as it was in the Garden of Eden between Adam, Eve, and God Himself, so it was between me and my son that day—another "voice" had apparently entered into Cole's life. Up until that very moment, my voice had been the only voice he had listened and responded to, and my way was the only way in Cole's mind. This was the very first moment Cole was introduced to another way of doing life other than Mommy's way. He was standing in the street, oblivious of the dangers, caught between the truth of my word and a lie. And he answered, "Well, Jaclyn said it was okay, Mommy. She plays in the street all the time, and she's not dead!"

After reprimanding him and sending him to his room, I went up later to talk to him. I simply told him, "Son, I discipline you because I care about you, and I set these boundaries because I want to protect you. And because I care about you so much, I have provided a huge backyard for you to play in that is much safer than the street!"

The same is true of God. That is why He has given us His "rules" and established boundaries for us—because He loves us, cares for us, and wants us to enjoy a long, healthy life free of the guilt, shame, and hurt that our choices—the choices made apart from His will—will bring. His way is the best way.

We can choose daily to walk after the spirit. We can choose to believe God and obey Him instead of the world and our fleshly desires. We can choose to listen only to the voice of God and follow after Truth even when our emotions are telling us to go the other way. We can choose to believe that God is with us even though we may not feel Him. We can choose to speak for Him, touch for Him, and walk with Him, even though we may not feel particularly anointed or able in the moment. And we can choose to get up and walk on when everything in life knocks us down. It may not be easy, but it is possible through Him.

CAUGHT IN THE MIDDLE

Choosing the Truth over the lie and faith over feelings is a great theory, but putting it into practice, I've found, isn't always so easy. You may ask, as I did, "How do I get past all of the negative thoughts and fears? How do I overcome my *feelings* and fleshly desires that steer me away from God and into destruction?"

Well, the first step is to identify the lies that we have fallen for in the past—acknowledging who or what experience convinced us of those lies; moreover, we must identify the feelings that led us to believe the lies. As we've established, emotions drive us, but we ultimately choose the destination. We must become aware of what those driving feelings are and where they are taking us.

For that very reason, I am asking you to take a first step of faith with me. If we're going to stop being led by our feelings and negative emotions, then we are going to have to identify them and "consider your ways!" as Haggai 1:5 says (NASB).

I want you to examine your thoughts now: What have you been focused on? God's Truth or the enemy's lie? Have you allowed someone, something, or life experience to become a "voice" in your ear, convincing you of the enemy's lie? What do you focus on throughout your day? Do you find yourself getting lost in hypothetical scenarios about something that may never come to pass? Do you find yourself dwelling on the past or wrapped up in the emotional memories of yesterday? Do you lose yourself in the imaginations of "what if" or "maybe one day"? Do you find yourself replaying conversations or rehearsing emotional events over and over again in your mind?

You might say, "Well, I've never thought about that. I have never really thought about what I think about!" Well, friend, if you have never thought about what you think about, then you ought to start now! It's not the will of God to have us mindlessly wandering through our days, being led by our emotions, our memories, our imaginations, and our own reasoning! His will is that we would be consciously following after His Spirit daily.

What if Adam and Eve had examined their thoughts in the garden that day? They probably would have discovered that bad information fed their thoughts, leading to feelings that ultimately drove them away from the will of God. And for that same reason, it is imperative that we stop to examine our own thoughts regularly. In fact, the psalmist David said, "Search me [thoroughly], O God, and know my heart! Try me and know my thoughts! And see if there is any wicked or hurtful way in me, and lead me in the way everlasting" (Ps. 139:23–24 AMP).

Recognizing and analyzing our thoughts is the only way to be sure that we are being led and driven by the Holy Spirit of God instead of the enemy. It is the only way to walk by faith instead of feelings.

WHAT I KNOW FOR CERTAIN

What I know for certain is that faith is not about what we can see, touch, hear, smell, or taste. Nor is it based on what we might be able to comprehend with our finite minds. It is, however, about what we choose to believe and in whom we choose to trust—by our own free will.

God's voice may not be audible to the human ear, His touch may not be felt in the same way you'd feel a pinch, and we may not be able to glimpse with our natural eyes God as He walks by, but what I do know is this: God is as real as you'll allow Him to be. He Himself is Truth, and He can be trusted. With a little bit of faith-filled vision, you can see Him daily in the beauty of the world around you—all you have to do is choose to see it. You can hear God through His Word or the words of a caring neighbor calling to check on you. You can feel God through the touch of a small child or the hands of a close friend. All you have to do is choose—choose to simply trust Him and take Him at His Word. Choose to believe in His love for you—regardless of what you might *feel*.

Walking in faith is always an active and deliberate choice. Choose daily to follow God's plan. While our senses can sometimes be wrong, His will can never be. We must remain obedient to His Word and His way of doing life.

> *God is as real as you'll allow Him to be.*

When we do, we will be filled with strong, grounded faith—a faith that has grown far beyond how we feel; it becomes what we believe, what we *know*. We become believers who are walking according to His will, by faith not by feelings.

No one ever asked us to *feel*...only to *believe*.

ACKNOWLEDGE IT

1. Do you find yourself falling prey to following after feelings over faith? Why?
2. In order to deal with them properly, identify some of the lies the enemy has convinced you of, especially the ones that trip you up daily. Begin by examining some of the feelings and beliefs you have about (a) God, (b) yourself, and (c) others.

    PLEASE don't skip this part. It is necessary to this process.

    Using index cards (or small pieces of paper), please answer the following questions, writing one answer on each card. (Leave the backs of the cards blank, and keep your cards handy. We'll use these again in chapter 6.)

    (a) What do you think about when you consider God and His character? What are some of the feelings you have about and toward God? Why? What event(s) convinced you of that belief?
    (b) What do you think about when you consider yourself or your life? Examine your heart. How do you honestly feel about yourself? Why? What event(s) convinced you of that belief?

(c) What are some of the thoughts you have toward others? Are you sometimes judgmental toward others or feel that people don't like you? What event(s) convinced you of those beliefs? Do you find yourself reading into things that people say or do? Why?

Now, tuck these answers away somewhere safe (even right here in your book). Give yourself a hand for your positive answers *and* for the honestly negative ones. Don't worry, we'll continue working past those negative mind-sets together.

3. Think about your thoughts: What are some of the external influences that affect your thoughts the most? Music? Movies? Magazines? Friends? Why do you think they have such an effect on you?

4. What can you do to keep your thought life more controlled so that you can focus more on God and His love for you?

Bring It to God

Lord, forgive me for trying to do life my own way. I know in my heart that Your way is the best way—help me to remember that. And thank You for teaching me that Your love for me is eternal and strong, regardless of what I may be feeling from day to day. Help me to trust more in that promise of Your love and to focus more on Your Truth rather than the enemy's lies. Help me to stay grounded in faith—anything else is just sinking sand!

Confess It

I will act on faith, not feelings.

I have followed the actions of Adam and Eve, allowing my feelings to determine my decisions, to sway me, to act apart from my faith, to separate me from God's perfect will. But that stops now.

I will no longer be moved by my feelings about myself or the world around me. I will guard the gateway into my soul by being mindful of my external influences and the emotions they provoke. I will think about what I am thinking about and will choose to follow faith-based emotions only.

Only God knows where I came from, where I stand now, and where I will be tomorrow. I am His, and He is mine. I cannot trust my feelings, but I will choose to trust my God.

My very next step will be one firmly grounded in faith.

Who ever asked you to feel?
You were chosen to be a princess!
Now go...
Wash your face...
Get a new attitude...
Put on your clothes...
And go be Cinderella!

CHAPTER 3

"You Were Chosen..."

PRINCESS PRINCIPLE #2:
TRUST GOD'S WISDOM IN CHOOSING YOU.

Trust in the LORD with all your heart
And do not lean on your own understanding.
~ PROVERBS 3:5 NASB

That day when Tommy spoke the words to me—"You were *chosen* to be a princess"—I have to tell you, everything inside of me wanted to scream, "That was your mistake, not mine!"

I was so looking for Tommy to admit the error in choosing me to be, of all things, a princess. In the heat of that moment, I was sure that confession would come gushing from his unbridled lips—a confession that would surely have pierced straight through my aching heart. But strangely enough, neither that day nor any other of my eight-month contract did Tommy ever admit or even insinuate that they may have made a mistake in choosing me.

For some reason, despite the many reasons I gave him to doubt me, he stood behind the choice they made following my audition.

I'll never forget the day I auditioned for the greatest entertainment company in the world. The position was entitled "Princess"…and the company, Disney!

After the audition, I stood nervously in front of the judges, anxiously awaiting their decision. While still under their scrutiny—either as an act of insanity or perhaps to *keep* myself sane—I proceeded to have a conversation with myself.

I'm doing it. I'm actually doing it! I can't believe I'm here. I've talked about it…but here I am! Okay, so I was dragged here kicking and screaming. But I am actually following through and am doing it.

Stop talking to yourself, Jennifer! Smile.

Wait. Can they see me shaking? My knees are knocking, and my lips keep sticking to my teeth. I look like an idiot.

But wait, if I do, then why are they staring at me so hard? What are they looking at? I think they're talking about me, but what could they be talking about for so long?

Okay, I think that lady just said something about my stomach. I knew I shouldn't have eaten yesterday!

How much longer could this take? I've either got it or I don't, right?

Ugh, it's been six whole minutes! Dear God, please don't let me pass out! My cheeks are twitching! I have to keep smiling…keep smiling.

Oh, just say it already. Call out my number: seventeen… seventeen…seventeen!

Okay, reality check: What are the odds? There are over a thousand girls, both here and in California, auditioning against me for the same six spots. Only six spots! What am I thinking? If they picked me, it wouldn't be a dream come true—it would be a miracle! Sixteen people were already shot down. Why would they pick me?

But you could be the first one...just wait! They're about to speak! Is it me? No way! Yes, way! Oh, come on! Say something already!

> *I wasn't a perfect princessy picture of grace and beauty.*

Then after what seemed like an eternity of waiting in silence, they spoke.

"Number seventeen, please step forward."

And that's how I was chosen.

Now exactly *why* I was chosen is beyond me. From my perspective, I was nothing that they were looking for. I wasn't a perfect princessy picture of grace and beauty. I was a tomboy whose throwing arm could rival most boys. And my skin was just too dark to portray any of those fair-skinned princesses. But I auditioned anyway—mostly because I drove my best friend there to the audition. When I discovered that it was possibly going to be a thirteen-hour-long audition, I figured that I might as well audition too. Besides, it had been my childhood dream.

I don't know what they saw in me that day. But they did. They saw what I couldn't see. In their eyes, they knew that I had *exactly* what it took to fill the roles of the Disney Princesses. But I was so wrapped up in myself, in my own insecurities, that I was completely unaware of what I had to offer and of their ability to transform ordinary, dark-skinned tomboys into graceful, ivory-skinned princesses. Despite my own doubts and fears, I was *chosen* to be a princess.

"EVERYTHING YOU NEED IS INSIDE THE BOX!"

On my very first day of work at Tokyo Disneyland, I stepped off the shuttle bus that picked us up in our village to bring us to work. As I did, I felt like I was stepping into a dream. We headed toward the greenroom, where we would spend the next eight months of our lives readying ourselves for each show or performance we would do.

Despite my own doubts and fears, I was chosen to be a princess.

As we filed one by one into the greenroom, Tommy handed each of us a box and instructed us to choose a vanity desk. It would be the place where we would keep our belongings and do our hair and makeup before each show. As he handed each of us our respective boxes, he made it a point to look us in the eye as he specifically spoke these words to each and every one of us: "Everything you need to be what you were called here to be is in that box. If it's not in there, you don't need it."

I chose the first desk to the right as I entered the room. It was next to a girl named Kim whom I'd met during the long flight over to Japan. I sat down on my chair, looked into that mirror for the first of probably a thousand times, and thought, *Wow, I'm really here. I am a Disney Princess!*

Before I could get carried away with my dream-come-true thoughts, I heard the other girls talking about all the great stuff in their boxes. So I immediately regained focus and tore into my box as well. As I opened the lid, I saw all kinds of neat dress-up materials. There were hair bows, makeup, gloves...and more makeup. *Free* makeup at that! As you can imagine, the room grew chaotic as we all began to comment on all the colors and tones we liked, as well as the ones we hated. But before long, our focus had shifted from the contents of our own box to that of each other's boxes.

I was quick to notice that every box was certainly *not* created equal. Nicole's box had a couple of things in it that I didn't have in my box, and some of the other girls had completely different stuff altogether! We all sat there comparing boxes until the room went from chaotic to absolute pandemonium.

Tommy came charging into the room. "*What* is going on in here?! What is the problem!?"

Of course I spoke up first, saying, "Well, Nicole's got some different things in her box than I have in mine. Ally over there has completely different stuff. And, well, I think I might be missing some stuff from my box!"

Tommy looked into my eyes and said something I will never forget. In utter frustration, he said, "What don't you understand? I told you that everything you need to be what you were called here to be is inside of that box. If it's not in there, you don't need it!"

EVERYTHING YOU NEED IS INSIDE OF YOU!

Tommy's frustration that day was triggered by our failure simply to trust that they, our superiors, knew full well what they were doing—not only when they chose us but when they compiled our necessities into our respective boxes. As a Disney Princess, those words didn't mean much more to me than the literal application of hair bows and makeup in a cardboard box. But Tommy's unintentional sermon that day held a profound truth that changed my perspective on trust, and I believe it will change you if you will grasp its reality:

*Everything you need to be what you were called here to be is
already inside of you.
And if it's not in there, you don't need it!*

I can imagine that God shares Tommy's same frustration. So
many times we fail to trust that He has perfectly equipped us with
all we need to fill our roles in this life—the roles that He Himself
has called us to, that He has chosen us for. We forget that *He* created the roles, and *He* created us. So what business do we have in
saying that we're ill equipped to fill those roles?

Today and every day, here in my life outside of Fantasyland, I
struggle to feel competent and equipped to perform in the multiple
roles I step into every day. But I can hear the Holy Spirit reminding
me that everything I need for this life is already inside of me. And
that means *everything*. We have all that we need.

ONE ROLE TO FILL

With all the many roles I was given to fill and all the many hats (or
should I say "wigs"?) I was given to wear, one of the most freeing
revelations of my life is that I, in fact, do not have to be excellent at
everything, and I don't have to possess every gift on this earth. I just
have to use the ones I *do have* with excellence.

And it's the same for *you*. God formed you on purpose for a
purpose, and He chose you to fill one specific role on this planet.
That role is just to be *you*! You're not required to be anybody else.
And no one is able to fill your role but you. You simply must learn
to trust the God who made you in order to fill it most effectively.

Even knowing that, I still must continually remind myself that
my one and only responsibility every day is to be the best *me* I can
possibly be. I do that by focusing on the gifts and talents that are

already inside of my "box." Sitting in the greenroom on that first day, I was quick to notice that all boxes were not the same. And I was right. The gifts in your box may differ from the gifts in my box, but that's perfectly all right. In fact, that's the way it's *supposed* to be. We are each created to have different features, gifts, talents, interests, and to serve individual purposes in this life.

We all come from different places and have different backgrounds. We all have our own set of challenges, trials, and temptations in life. We all have our own stories. That is God's plan. Different people can reach different kinds of people—we just have to come to trust His plan.

GET A LITTLE GOD-PERSPECTIVE

Just as I wondered at Disney's reasons behind choosing me, I have also wondered at God's. Couldn't He have chosen a more perfect mother? Someone better suited for ministry? A more articulate author? And the answer, I've learned, is *no*. I'm sure I'll never fully understand God's reasoning this side of heaven, but I've found that it helps to speed up the process tremendously if I use a little God-perspective.

Looking at myself on that Disney stage, I would have seen a girl with an empty box—or at least a girl with a box full of junk. But my box is not empty. It never was. And neither is yours.

It's all a matter of perspective.

For God, it's easy. He is privy to the big picture. He knows all of the ins and outs and end results of His intentional, perfect design. But since our limited human capacity doesn't comprehend the enormity of God's plan, we must first remember not to lean upon our own understanding (see Prov. 3:5–6). Then, we must do these two things in order to gain His perspective: We must first come to know Him and then come to trust Him. Doing the first will automatically lead to the second, once you come to know God for who He truly is.

To go beyond simply knowing *of* Him and becoming intimate and personal *with* Him, we must come to know His character and His will concerning us. When you get to know God and His character in a more intimate way, you become aware of His perspective and what He is all about. When you don't know Him, it makes it all the easier for you to believe the enemy's lies about God—like when the enemy causes you to feel like God is mad at you for something you've done. Or the moments when the enemy causes you to feel like God has given up on you. And even when the enemy tells you that you're not equipped to fulfill God's purpose. Those are just falsehoods that the enemy has created to test and tempt you, to topple your faith.

We must first come to know Him and then come to trust Him.

How do I know? Simply because the Bible tells me so and, more specifically, because I know that it is not the character of God to quit on someone who makes a mistake. I know Him personally; I have come to know more and more about His character. And when you develop a strong relationship with Him, it makes it all the easier to shut up the enemy and to focus on *God's* perspective concerning you.

King David learned much about God's character in his lifetime. By the time he wrote the Psalms, he had gained an amazing perspective about God's relationship with us. The words penned by King David tell us: "For you created my inmost being; you knit me together in my mother's womb. I praise you because I am fearfully and wonderfully made; your works are wonderful, I know that full well" (Ps. 139:13–14).

That portion of Scripture is a very familiar one, especially to us as women. It is a Scripture that I am asked to teach from when I get invited to conferences to speak on the subject of identity, beauty, and purpose. I love those subjects, but more often than not, I enter the conference hall with the full understanding that most women and girls don't actually believe that they're beautiful, wonderful, or perfectly created just as they are. I know because for the longest time, I didn't believe it either.

I mean, come on, when is the last time you looked in the mirror and said, "I am beautiful. I am perfectly and wonderfully created, and I love everything about me"?

Yeah, that didn't happen much in my house either—at least not without trying. But it's the truth. And real Truth is what God says whether it agrees with the world's view or not, whether or not we see it, feel it, or understand it.

King David knows "full well" that he is perfectly, wonderfully, amazingly made.

Do you?

Are you convinced that you are fearfully, specifically, and wonderfully made by God? That *you* are an amazing creation of God Himself? Do you actually, undoubtedly believe that?

Well, according to God, we should!

So what keeps us from believing it? What keeps us from *knowing* that we truly are what and who God says we are? Is it our flaws? Our imperfections? Our issues? Our differences?

What keeps us from seeing beauty within ourselves? Is it our deformities? Our thigh size? Our large, protruding ears? Our crooked teeth and freckles? Our awkwardness?

Who told you that you were not wonderfully amazing? It certainly wasn't God. So whoever it was, they were lying, speaking against God's Truth.

Let's see what we can do to get a little God-perspective.

The rest of the passage from Psalm 139 goes like this:

> *Oh yes, you shaped me first inside, then out;*
>   *you formed me in my mother's womb.*
> *I thank you, High God—you're breathtaking!*
>   *Body and soul, I am marvelously made!*
>   *I worship in adoration—what a creation!*
> *You know me inside and out,*
>   *you know every bone in my body;*
> *You know exactly how I was made, bit by bit,*
>   *how I was sculpted from nothing into something.*
> *Like an open book, you watched me grow from conception to birth;*
>   *all the stages of my life were spread out before you,*
> *The days of my life all prepared*
>   *before I'd even lived one day.* (vv. 13–16 MSG)

Wow. Now, there's a Truth to grasp. David emphatically declares just how intimately God knows us, how intricately He was involved in forming us, and how interested He is in being the biggest and best part of our lives. David had that kind of relationship with God. He trusted God and His character fully—so much so that when David was going through a very painful and difficult period in his life, the Bible says that "David strengthened himself with trust in his GOD" (1 Sam. 30:6 MSG). David so clearly demonstrates that only when we come to fully comprehend *whose* we are, can we fully embrace *who* we are.

> *When we fully comprehend whose we are, we can fully embrace who we are.*

We are His workmanship, and we are wonderful. Yes! We are! That means you and me! You see, the world's view is that we are only priceless if we are perfect, but God's view is that we are perfect *because* we are priceless. He bought our perfection with the very precious, priceless blood of His very own Son, Jesus. And while I realize that, sure, there may be things about us that could use improvement, our loving Heavenly Father views us to be perfect because we are His! We simply need to meditate on this Truth until we begin to see things the way He does.

You've already convinced yourself of your current belief system, right? You believe what you believe because you input information and then came into agreement with it. *Someone or something* came along and convinced you of it—just as it happened with Adam and Eve in the garden. You agreed with the world's lies, the misconceptions of beauty and perfection, and it eventually became your truth—not *the* Truth, but your truth. Now, you just have to choose to begin inputting new, *truthful* information that lines up with God's Word. You have to choose to trust God at His Word.

Think of it as reprogramming your mind's computer. If you begin by identifying then deleting the improper information and begin to input correct information in its place (and we'll do more of this in chapter 6), sooner or later your mind will be restored. Once it is restored, you can then draw on that proper information to gain a proper perspective to live life to its fullest. This new Truth, God's Truth, becomes your strong foundation on which you stand to gain His perspective.

But, the thing is, you must determine to convince yourself of it *daily*, on *purpose*. It doesn't happen by accident. And it isn't always easy.

THE UNCHANGEABLES

For years, instead of looking in the mirror to see all the things I liked about myself, I found it much easier to notice all the things I hated about me. (Hmm, you too?) And I made no bones about saying it out loud to myself either. It got to the point where all I could see—every time I examined myself or my life—was the negative. God eventually revealed to me that every time I criticized myself, I was also criticizing Him. He was my Creator, my Designer. I never intended to offend Him, but I did.

God revealed to me that every time I criticized myself, I was also criticizing Him.

Now, self-examination is not *always* a bad thing. Some of my self-examination led me to make positive changes in my attitude, my eating habits, and my behavior. The problem arose when I was displeased with things that I could not change, that I had no control over.

A powerful teaching by Bill Gothard and the Institute in Basic Life Principles helped me to build trust in my God, my Designer, and to accept *all* of me, even the things I had always wished I could change. The framework of this powerful teaching led me—and millions of others—to accept what Gothard calls the unchangeables.[1]

1. Physical Features
2. Parents
3. Gender
4. Brothers and Sisters
5. Birth Order
6. Ethnicity

7. Place of Origin
8. Time in History
9. Mental Capacity
10. Aging and Time of Death

Any of those on your list of "Things I'd Like to Change About Myself"? Yeah, me too. But please, do as Bill Gothard teaches and "choose to be grateful for God's purposes for these unchangeable features."[2] *Acceptance* means that we relinquish control over trying to change the circumstance. You will come to find that accepting God's design and having faith and trust in His plan for your life will bring about peace as you begin to cooperate with—instead of struggle *against*—all that He desires to fulfill in your life.

Whether we can see it or not, from God's all-knowing perspective, we were predestined (see Eph. 1:5), perfectly designed, with those "gifts"— those unchangeables—in mind. It was all God's *intentional, perfect* design.

Accepting God's design will bring about peace.

In Jeremiah 29:11, God tells us, "I know what I'm doing. I have it all planned out—plans to take care of you, not abandon you, plans to give you the future you hope for." (MSG) But we have to choose to trust Him.

Okay, so you're thinking, *Great theory, Jennifer. Now, what does this look like in* real *life?* Well, I'll give you a personal example of the first "unchangeable"—physical features—with a truly God-given purpose.

My entire life I have had a very athletic build. I would have much rather been stick, bean-pole skinny. But no such luck. I'm guessing since birth I've had these big, muscular legs that have bodybuilder potential—especially my huge, honkin' calves. In college, I always got comments from guys in the gym asking me what I do to grow my calves. My answer was always, "Nothing—you want them?!"

In my post-Disney days, I was working for a marketing company doing sales presentations and training. The skirts and heels I wore while speaking naturally made my calves look even bigger. After one particular presentation, one of the audience members approached me and asked if he could pay me a compliment. He was a young, attractive guy in his twenties, so I said, "Sure!" The first words out of his mouth were, "You've got grrreat calves!"

That guy's name was Anthony Beckham, and I married him eight weeks later! We've been married for fourteen years now with two children, and he is still a self-proclaimed "calf man." Of all the body parts that he has always found most attractive on a woman, big, muscular calves have always been on the top of his list. There's not a day that goes by that he doesn't follow me up the stairs to catch a glimpse of my flexing calves as I walk.

Sound silly? Maybe, but it's a constant reminder to me that God knew full well what He was doing when He formed me in my mother's womb. I had always thought that God made a huge mistake when He slapped these things on the backs of my legs. Little did I know, when He was forming me in my mother's womb, He had already formed a little boy named Anthony in his mother's womb, giving him an innate love for big, strong calves. God truly does know what He's doing—even if it took me twenty-one years to discover it!

Now, what if that physical feature is a limitation, a genetic issue, or a birth defect? What do we do with that?

Well, again, it's all a matter of perspective.

The apostle Paul tells us that he was given a thorn in the flesh, or as *The Message* says, he was given the "gift of a handicap" to keep him in constant touch with his limitations (see 2 Cor. 12:7). What a perspective!

In verse 8 he says that he pleaded with the Lord three different times to deliver him of the issue. But God chose not to. Instead, God's answer to Paul in verse 9 was, "My grace is sufficient for you, for my power is made perfect in weakness." Paul had to choose to trust.

Paul was given the "gift of a handicap."

In Exodus 4:10, we learn that Moses had a speech problem. Yet instead of healing him, God chose to use Moses just as he was. In the story of the blind man in John 9:1, we find out that Jesus said that this man was born blind to display the work of God in his life.

Sometimes through the dynamic strength required to overcome physical limitations, you can build a platform from which you can touch the world. Take Nick Vujicic for example. According to his website, this Australian was born December 4, 1982, to two devoted Christian parents who pastored a local church. Nick was pronounced a healthy baby with one exception: He had no limbs, only a vestigial left foot that now allows him to bounce, balance, and navigate his customized wheelchair. This "limitation" doesn't limit him at all; in fact, people are drawn to him because of it, and he travels all over the world ministering to millions about the love and goodness of God.[3]

Check out his website (www.lifewithoutlimbs.org) or videos on YouTube, and you'll be instantly astounded by him and his outlook on life. Nick himself admits that it was not always easy for him and his family to see the purpose of his physical condition. However, with spiritual maturity and a fresh perspective from God, Nick is now fully convinced that God's glory is revealed through him. "He uses me just the way I am," he says. "And even more wonderful, He can use me in ways others can't be used."[4]

Nick's mantra is "From life without limbs to life without limits!" He is totally independent, college-educated, a motivational speaker, evangelist, real-estate and stock-market investor, and author. Nick says that God instilled a "passion of sharing my story and experiences to help others cope with whatever challenge they might have in their lives. Turning my struggles into something that would glorify God and bless others, I realized my purpose! The Lord was going to use me to encourage and inspire others to live to their fullest potential and not let anything get in the way of accomplishing their hopes and dreams." [5]

Nick Vujicic has chosen to see God's perspective on his life, and so can we.

Many who have faced challenges and setbacks because of ethnicity and place of origin (unchangeables six and seven) have chosen that same God-perspective. God used Esther's race and nationality to put her in a place where she spared all of her own people from holocaust. In the modern-day world, Martin Luther King, Jr. rose up among his people and promoted change.

The choice is yours. You can either despise your ethnicity and your nationality because of the hardships it may cause, or you can choose to use it to make needed changes within yourself and within your community.

Regarding mental capacity (number nine), sure, we can study to improve our learning. But for the most part, we have been blessed with different learning styles and the capacity to understand different subjects. And that's okay. Some of us are called to be rocket scientists, engineers, or mathematicians. Others fill the needed roles of actors, pianists, and musicians. Learn to accept your capacities and then find the best place to use what God has given to you.

What about the gift of family (numbers two and four)? Whether it's our generous Aunt Martha or our weird Uncle Alfred, family can seem like both a blessing and a curse. But keep in mind that while we cannot change them, we can choose whether or not to become like them.

In the story of the young King Josiah, found in 2 Kings, we see that Josiah was given rule over Judah and Jerusalem at the very young age of eight. His father, Amon, the fifteenth ruler of Judah, was killed by his own servants after only two years of his reign. Both Josiah's father and grandfather, Manasseh, were terribly wicked kings. But it was the grandfather who was given the credit of being the *most* wicked king in Judah's history after he desecrated the sacred things of the Lord and sacrificed his own son to the idol Molech.

When Josiah came to rule, he inherited a nation in ruins. Thanks to his father and grandfather, there were idolatrous priests, people practicing sodomy and prostitution inside the temple of God, soothsaying, astrological worship, and the ritual sacrifice of children. Talk about a horrible inheritance! At eight years old, Josiah had his little hands full and could have easily chosen to continue in his ancestors' footsteps.

At the age of sixteen, Josiah began seeking hard after the Lord. At the age of twenty, he got radical with his faith and purged the lands he ruled of all their heathen idols and tore down every altar where other gods were worshipped. Then, at the age of twenty-six, while he was in the process of repairing the temple, Josiah's priest uncovered the Book of the Law—or God's Word. Immediately after reading it, Josiah chose to repent to the Lord and called a national assembly to renew Judah's commitment and covenant with God. He decided to turn his country around for the honor of God.

The task he had inherited from his wicked father and grandfather was a huge one, but in the end he eliminated idolatry and pagan worship and established much good for God. Judah was blessed by God under Josiah's rule with the last great revival. Second Kings tells us, "There was no king to compare with Josiah—neither before nor after—a king who turned in total and repentant obedience to

GOD, heart and mind and strength....The world would never again see a king like Josiah" (2 Kings 23:25 MSG).

Josiah chose his own course—and God's course—in spite of his inheritance. And King David did too; he says in Psalm 27:10, "Although my father and my mother have forsaken me, yet the Lord will take me up [adopt me as His child]" (AMP).

Your gender, your time in history, and your lifespan (unchangeables three, eight, and ten) are all a part of God's plan, too, if you will but trust God. It's the same for birth order (number five). In fact, our birth order helps to develop our very personalities that we will use to reach the people to whom we are sent. Firstborn children have been said to have a greater capacity to lead and respond to order, whereas middle children tend to be more loyal and competitive. Lastborn children are said to be more independent and persuasive. Which one are you? Whichever you are, trust that God chose your birth order knowing full well that it would help to shape the very personality that He will use to reach others and through which He will accomplish great things.

TWO INDISPENSABLE UNCHANGEABLES

I would like to add two more unchangeables I believe belong on this list: our giftings and our past. These, too, are things we cannot change no matter how hard we try, but like all of the others, they require the proper perspective in order to accept and appreciate them.

I have come to understand, through a trust in God, that there are gifts and talents that I do not and will not ever possess, and that's all right. If I needed them and were meant to use them, then certainly, God would have given them to me! (You may want to read that again for yourself. Let it sink in deep!) If we will just learn to keep our eyes in our own boxes—the boxes with *everything* we need to fulfill our God-given roles—and discover, cultivate, and use those unique gifts given to each of us, imagine the wonderful things we would accomplish for God, the giver of all gifts (see James 1:17)! And imagine how content and fulfilled we would feel as a result.

And our past—*whew!* Wouldn't we all love to go back and change *something* about our past? There's not one of us who hasn't done something we wish we could take back, rewind, or do over. We have all made mistakes and we have all experienced pain and hurt in our past that we'd like to forget. I call all those things "ugly gifts," and boy did I have a lot of them in my box! But from God's perspective, our past is a treasure trove from which to pull great lessons and experience. Our past holds stories that begin with, "You know, I've been there, and I can tell you with confidence..." Those are mistakes that we can point back to that serve as lessons learned or even inspiration for others. "Hang in there. I did the same thing, and I made it through okay." No, you can't change your past, but you *can* get a God-perspective to see what's back there for you to use for God's glory. (More on that later.)

Whether it be a "pretty" gift, such as a beautiful singing voice or great leadership qualities, or an "ugly gift" such as pain and shame from a past you'd like to erase, everything we have right here, right now, can be used for God's glory.

Let it all speak.

Every voice, every experience, every pain, every mistake, and every single scar—they will all speak if we'll let them, if we give our purposes over to God and allow Him to speak through us.

We have everything we need to be the princesses God has chosen us to be. Above all, we have God. And we can do all things through Him. Our abilities lie not in our own hands, but in His. Let us not ever forget His amazing ability to fill our flaws with His grace and glory—or as John 9 explains, so that the works of God might be revealed through us. Where we fall short, He steps in and shines through us. In fact, the greater our flaws, the further He brings us to overcome them and the brighter His glory shines through.

We can trust Him to shine through every time. In fact, we *must* trust Him if we are going to choose to keep walking in faith. *That* is our main job in this life—to trust, rely on, and cleave to our God.

The bottom line? It's not about us. *It is all about God.* He created us. He has a plan for us. He has *chosen* us, with all of our imperfections and differences, to participate in that perfect plan. The sooner we realize that, the sooner we can get on with His purpose for our lives.

ACKNOWLEDGE IT

1. Do you struggle to believe that you are fearfully and wonderfully made? Why?
2. What, if anything, would you love to change about yourself or your life? Why?
3. What do you think God's perspective is on those things you would change?
4. After reading this chapter, can you see some areas where you need to learn to trust God more? What can you do to accomplish this?

5. Since perspective is everything, can you now name three things you like about yourself that you can begin focusing on and thanking God for?

Bring It to God

Lord, forgive me for not trusting You more. I know now that the more I come to truly know You, the more I will be able to trust You. Help me to know You and Your character better by spending more time with You through prayer and in the study of Your Word. That's what I want: to know You more, to trust You completely, and to see myself and my life from Your perspective. Help me, Lord, to accept myself and Your plan for my life, even when it doesn't make total sense to me. My life is in Your hands.

Confess It

I will trust God's wisdom in choosing me for His purpose.

I have no idea why God, the omnipotent Creator of the universe, has chosen me. But I know that He has.

I know that I cannot fully appreciate my imperfections without God's perspective. But I choose now to accept them. I will even be grateful for my flaws and imperfections because I know that they will allow God's glory to shine through to the world.

I don't know exactly why I was where I was, why I am where I am, or why I will be where I will be. But right now, I accept my past, present, and future as part of God's perfect plan.

From this point forward, I will make a concerted effort to further my relationship with God, to learn more of His character. I know that as a result I will gain wisdom about His perspective and gain understanding about the purpose He has for my life.

I am chosen. I have a purpose. And I am His. I need nothing else.

Who ever asked you to feel?
You were chosen to be a princess!
Now go...
Wash your face...
Get a new attitude...
Put on your clothes...
And go be Cinderella!

CHAPTER 4

"Go!"

PRINCESS PRINCIPLE #3:
ALLOW GOD TO HEAL THE TENDER PLACES
IN YOUR LIFE.

Therefore, confess your sins to one another...so
that you may be healed.

~ JAMES 5:16 NASB

After Tommy spoke those harsh words to me that fateful morning at Disney, I was dumbfounded. I stood speechlessly frozen to the spot—that was until Tommy adamantly pointed his finger toward the greenroom door, repeating sternly, "Go!"

Though completely devastated inside, I didn't have the time or the emotional wherewithal even to consider doing anything more than what I'd been ordered to do. I had to *go.*

I hurried over to my locker and snatched my Cinderella bloomers and a towel, knowing full well that my first stop would be the restroom where I could sob out my anguish without everyone knowing about it. Pulling the door handle, I opened the heavy metal door just enough for me to sneak through. I scampered down the hallway with my head down, refusing to make eye contact with anyone.

All the way down the hall, I did my best to hold it in. I was embarrassed, hurt, and angry—and not just because of Tommy. At this point, I was feeling every ounce of pain, frustration, hurt, and rejection that had ever been inflicted upon me. And with every step toward the bathroom, I just knew that my tears, my hurt, and my anger would explode, exposing all to the world. Somehow I had maintained my composure this far.

Then, when I was just steps away from the restroom, a friend and Japanese coworker stepped into my path. "Hello, friend!" she chirped.

Ugh, I groaned inwardly. If there ever was a time I didn't want to hear those words, it was at that moment. However, I quickly looked up and answered back, "Hi, Tan-ji." I faked my best smile.

And when she continued, "You don't look so happy today," I smiled a little harder. I don't remember the full extent of our conversation, but I do recall changing the subject every time she asked, "Are you sure you're okay?"

Just before walking away, Tan-ji reminded me that she was my friend. She assured me that she was there for me if I ever needed to talk. But I just smiled through my pain and looked away.

BITING MY LIP

I spent most of my life doing just that—running and hiding from whatever pain I was facing. A vivid memory from my childhood tells me it was something I learned at a very early age.

One afternoon, I was playing out in my front yard while our neighbor was outside washing his car. Always in need of attention, I decided to show off by doing some gymnastics. On my fourth cartwheel in a row, my foot came down into a thorny tree that deposited about thirty full-size thorns into my foot. I ran to my garage without making a sound, but once inside I began screaming and crying for help.

Help came in the form of my parents. Together they held me down as my mom began to pull each thorn, one by one, from my foot. It was excruciating.

My dad told me to bite down on my bottom lip. "You won't feel the pain in your foot so bad." I did as he suggested, and he was right. The pain from biting my lip was enough to take my mind off of the pain of the original wound.

Don't we all do that? Instead of dealing with the pain at hand, facing it head-on, we create more drama and distractions, welcoming more pain into our lives, in order to mask the original pain that just needs to be dealt with once and for all. Like me, that day in the hallway at Tokyo Disneyland, we look away, smile, or bite our lips, all the while denying that something is really wrong. How clever we think we are at masking our pain.

How clever we think we are at masking our pain.

And it's not just you or me, sister. We're *all* guilty. As far back as biblical times, we've tried to hold our heads high despite the truths weighing down our hearts. Remember the woman at the well from John chapter 4? Her story is one of my favorites in the entire Bible. Married five times and living with the sixth man, she certainly had some burdens to bear. Let's look at her story.

We know that the woman at the well was a Samaritan woman in a day where women were considered to be "property" and

Samaritans, well, they were considered to be "half-breeds" and traitors to God's people. For this reason, Jews of the day despised them and purposefully steered clear from them and their land at all costs. (Well, except for Jesus, of course, who was there on an assignment from His Heavenly Father.)

For all intents and purposes, the Samaritan woman was an outcast—and for more reasons than those we named already. Her reputation alone was enough to deem her disgraceful. Married five times and now shacked up with her sixth man, it was safe to say she was not at all respected among her peers. And being that she was such a "hit" with the men probably made her all the more hated among the women.

We also find out, with a bit of research, that there was actually a well closer to the village where the woman lived. For some reason, she bypassed that well and went out of her way to go to the well further from her village. Secondly, she had come to the well alone. Studies of the culture of that day show that women usually went together to the well. (Ever gone to the bathroom with a flock of women? We haven't changed a bit.) And they went later in the day when it was cooler. Yet this woman came *alone*, during the heat of the day.

The Bible doesn't go into detail, but perhaps she bypassed her nearby well and went to the farther well at an "off" hour of the day because she was avoiding someone or something that was closer to home. I imagine the scorching sun was nothing compared to the vicious tongues of those women who despised her. Or maybe the wounds of her past and her reputation made it too uncomfortable to be around other people. Perhaps it was just easier to be alone rather than continuing to pretend everything was fine or to ignore the remarks others were making about her. Maybe being alone was better than putting on that mask in front of others. Whatever her reason, she was by herself the day she encountered Jesus.

By all evidence, the woman at the well fits the description of a woman with a past full of pain, searching for fulfillment and a quick fix for her emptiness. When she stumbles upon Jesus at the well, in their brief conversation, she even asks Him to give her a drink of the water He spoke of, so she wouldn't have to thirst anymore. Undoubtedly, she was thirsty for love, acceptance, and respect.

She was thirsty for love, acceptance, and respect.

But instead of Jesus appeasing her and simply meeting her every need, He went *there*.

"Go..." He instructs. More specifically, "Go and get your husband" (John 4:16 NLT). Yeowch!

He addressed and prodded the tender, gaping wounds that she'd rather just be forgotten. The reason? He loved her way too much to become another quick fix for her deep-seated issues.

THIS WILL ONLY HURT FOR A SECOND

When the woman at the well tells Jesus, "I have no husband," Jesus simply agrees with her. "You are right....The fact is, you have had five husbands, and the man you now have is not your husband. What you have just said is quite true" (John 4:17-18). Notice that Jesus wanted her to not only acknowledge the condition of her life right now, but to also recognize the patterns in her life leading up to that moment in time.

If Jesus already knew this, why would He give such an instruction? And why would He have gone out of His way to be there at that well at noon strategically to meet with this woman, only to then dig up her painful past and shine such a light on this area of her private, personal life?

Jesus had a specific plan for her life, but before she could real-ize it, He needed her to examine her situation. He wanted her to stop biting her lip to distract herself from her wound. Jesus knew that sometimes the only way to move forward is to go back—back to the place where the wounds were initially inflicted, back to the place where you *first* learned how to look away and deny the pain.

Likewise when God asks us a question or gives us instruction, it's not for Him. It's not so that *He* can learn something—it's so that *we* can.

When God asked Adam after he'd eaten from the Tree of Knowledge of Good and Evil, "Where are you, Adam?" it wasn't because God wanted to know where Adam was; He already knew. He wanted Adam to recognize where he was. After Cain killed his brother Abel, God asked him, "Where is your brother? Where is Abel?" God knew exactly what Cain had done, and He knew about the jealousy in Cain's heart that had driven him to it. He just wanted Cain to recognize it.

As with Adam and Cain and the woman at the well, we all have issues in our lives. We have wounds that need some attention. Sure we say that 'time heals all wounds', but does it really? The truth is: time may have moved on, but the pain is still very present. For many of us, that wound has festered and become infected. We've bandaged it; we've covered it over. But it's there, and it hurts. It's tender to the touch. If someone accidentally bumps into us where we've been wounded, they regret it. And we want just to leave it alone, deny the incident ever happened—because honestly, the nec-essary procedure for proper healing of the wound would be much too painful.

Unfortunately, that painful process is essential to proper healing.

In the medical field, when someone is brought in with a wound that is infected, it is sliced open so that it may heal from the inside out. And that's just what Jesus did to the woman at the well. He didn't skirt around the issue. He went straight to the heart of the matter. He sliced the wound open—not to be malicious or to compound her pain, but so that she would heal. From the inside out.

You see, Jesus had good reason for this divine appointment. He had gone to Samaria to reap a harvest of souls and to impact the lives of the Samaritan people. The woman at the well was chosen as the one Jesus would use to do it. After she met Jesus and was ultimately healed by His unconditional love and acceptance, she would then go on to introduce Jesus to her entire community in Samaria. She found her purpose—but only after she was willing to go back and address the painful wounds from her past.

If you were to meet Jesus at the well, what would your conversation be? What wounds would He be gracious enough to slice open? Are there self-inflicted wounds in your past? Decisions and actions that you're less than proud of? Or has someone wounded you? Were you a victim of wrongs against you that were always too painful to face or confess? Regardless of the mode of delivery, those wounds can be healed. They *must* be healed for you to continue in the purpose God has for you.

Please understand, if you are among the "walking wounded" who appear to be healthy and well-functioning but are, in all actuality, all banged up and broken on the inside, then you must go back and identify those events that caused you internal damage and changed the course of your life. Make no mistake about it: Every event that has caused emotional turmoil within you has formed attitudes, memories, and belief systems that have led you to where you are now—bound by yesterday and unable to experience the joys of today. You must go back to discover and to finally deal with the emotional strongholds of your life. You may have to go back in time a week, a month, or a year ago to when your heart was ripped open by that betrayal you didn't see coming. Or you may have to go back as many as ten, twenty, or even thirty years to that moment when your life was forever changed by some selfish, deceived individual who chose not to consider anyone's feelings but his own. But no matter what the event or how much time has lapsed since then, take courage, my friend. If God is calling you back to address the wounds of your past, then He is fully committed to heal them with His unfailing love.

You don't have to walk to the well. Jesus is waiting for you. He wants to meet you right here, right now, and offer healing for that festering, painful injury from your past. All you have to do is acknowledge the wound and offer it for His healing.

TELL HIM EVERYTHING

My woman-at-the-well experience came out of nowhere. I had been married to my husband for over a year, and my relationship with him—along with every other loved one in my life—was struggling. It became apparent that the issues of my past—the ones I had hoped to forget—were plaguing my newfound life. I was jealous, angry, bitter, and resentful, finding it difficult to cover up the gaping holes and the deep-seated issues of my past failures and rejections. I could not go on pretending that my past was in my past; it was very much a part of my present.

One night in Yulee, Florida, after preaching a revival service with my husband, Anthony, I lay sleeplessly in bed with the realization that something desperately needed to change. Then God began dealing with my heart. *Tell him everything!*

Everything? No, God, not everything, my heart answered back. *He'd never forgive me and he...he wouldn't love me anymore, God! Please, no!*

Tell him everything. Leave nothing out. Now. It's time.

I tried to reason that opening up my past during this time of spiritual revival would surely be detrimental to what we were trying to accomplish in that city. Ultimately trying to play "Let's Make a Deal" with God, I tried my last excuse.

God, You know how cranky he gets when I wake him up out of a dead sleep. Maybe it'd be best to tell him this stuff in the morning...

Just then, to my amazement, Anthony rolled over in the bed and let out a huge sigh. "I can't sleep!" he said in frustration.

Okay, so God was obviously not in the mood for making deals. I reasoned to myself that it was probably better to get this over with now anyway. *I suppose I always knew this time would have to come,* I said to myself.

So I sat up in bed, told my husband I needed to talk, and conceded to God's command to share every gory detail of my hideous past with the one person I desperately did not want to tell.

Let's just say that my life before meeting my husband, Anthony, was one I am certainly not proud of. I desperately sought love to fill the hole left in my heart by my father's death. I had given myself to anyone who gave me the attention I needed to forget about the pain. I attached myself to anyone who said they loved me, and soon I began settling for anyone who seemed like they could come to love me...one day...maybe. I was pathetic.

But as far as Anthony was concerned, I was an angel. Like most men, Anthony wanted to believe that the woman he had fallen in love with was spotless and pure. That was the one thing I certainly was not. But I was very happy to oblige his belief. I kept all of my past right there—in my past—telling him nothing, with the fear that if he ever came to find out, he'd surely never love me or want me.

You see, Anthony was my best chance to start over with a clean slate. And I was so ready that I married him exactly eight short weeks after meeting him. (Talk about your quick fixes!) I *ran* to the opportunity to leave my past in the past and never look back.

So now there it was, nearly three o'clock in the morning and one year into our very rocky and tumultuous marriage (thanks to my anger, jealousy, and rejection issues). And I was about to bare my soul to the man who had given me my first glimpse of a positive future. I was terrified.

Digging up my past and laying it at my husband's feet was sure to hurt him and was sure to change everything. But God had made it clear that I had no other choice, and frankly, I was more than ready to get it over with. The only thing left for me to do was trust—trust that if God Himself directed me to do it, there must be a good reason why He would put me through the agony of revisiting my very painful past and taking my husband with me.

"*I just can't live like this anymore.*"

So I cleared my voice and began to speak.

"There are some things about me, about my past, that I have to tell you. I realize that what I'm about to say may change everything, but...I just can't live like this anymore."

By that point, we were both propped up against the bed's backboard in the very dark room. I kept my head down as I spoke so as to not look at his face, afraid of what I might see. Knowing what I was about to share with him, and not knowing how he would react, I braced myself for just about anything.

I uncovered every dreadful piece of my past life. All the things I'd done, and all the places I'd been, all the people I'd been with prior to my meeting him. I used wisdom in the things I was sharing, trying not to cause him pain but doing my best to reveal what God wanted me to reveal. Everything I was sharing was everything he never wanted to know. It was everything both of us wanted to pretend would never affect our marriage but undeniably was.

Looking up, I could see half of his face from the streetlight that shone through the slats of the plantation shutters. There were times that I could see him gritting his teeth, wrenching the covers, and squeezing his fists until his knuckles turned white. During other parts of my confession, I could feel his heaving breaths, see him wiping tears from his eyes and biting his lip to keep him from responding to my words—all the while keeping completely silent.

With the entirety of my past laid out before him, I waited in complete silence for him to say something, anything. I'm sure he didn't know what to say, and to be honest, I don't know what I wanted to hear. I think part of me would have found it easier to be left alone in the shame that I had grown so accustomed to living with. I well deserved to be called every name in the book for not letting him know up front who and what he was marry-ing—especially since he was called to be a minister of God's holy Word. I not only deserved but *expected* that he would look at me in disgust, tell me things could never be the same between us, and then leave me to sleep alone in my tears. The only thing that brought me a trickle of relief was that it was almost over. I could end the façade and stop living my life as an imposter.

I couldn't bear the silence one more second. I braced myself one last time and finally said, "Please…say something!"

It took everything I had to look his way, but when I did I could see him reach up and wipe another tear from his eye. He looked into my eyes and responded in a way I never would have expected and certainly never, ever could have deserved.

He said, "I love you."

After another moment of silence, he reached over and wrapped his massive arms around me, giving me a safe place to let it all out. As I began to cry, streams of tears became oceans of grief and deep shame. He said again, "I love you so much, and I am so sorry that they hurt you like that."

That night we cried and held each other for several hours, crying until there were no tears left to cry. I remember weeping over Anthony's response to my sin, realizing that I was in the arms of a godly man who could have withheld his love from me, held it against me, or left me alone, unforgiven and further ashamed of my past life. As he held me, I thought of all the things he could have said and could have done but didn't.

Then in an instant, my thoughts shifted, and I began to shed tears for an entirely different reason. Thinking of Anthony's response, of the unconditional grace and forgiveness he had just shown me, I began thanking God for this incredibly amazing man that He had given to me. Then I heard something from God that completely broke through the wall that I had built up around my heart. He said to me, This *is how I love you*. This *is how I receive you*. This *is how I respond to you and your past*.

Just as I had expected, that one event in my life did change everything. It changed my relationship with my husband. It changed my relationship with the Lord. It changed my relationship with myself. What I hadn't expected is that it changed it all *for the better*.

God already knew everything about me. My husband may not have known, but God knew. And I knew. Everything I knew about myself was eating me up inside. Every failure, every event convinced me that I was not good enough, not worthy of love, and not fully accepted. And what was going on inside of me was quickly manifesting itself on the outside of me. I had been living my life in complete fear, not only feeling but *acting* like I was unlovely, unlovable, and unworthy of anything good this life had to offer. I was unknowingly sabotaging every relationship that God was trying to bless me with, in fear that if they got too close to me, they'd discover me for who I truly was and reject me. (Perhaps that's why the woman at the well had been married five times.)

Confession Brings Healing

I didn't realize it at the time, but God's command to confess my lies, my failures, and my sins was acting out a powerful Scripture that says, "Therefore, confess your sins to one another…so that you may be healed" (James 5:16 NASB).

I know what you're thinking. How could telling someone about your sins, your faults, your weaknesses, or your mistakes actually bring healing?

Confession is our sign of surrender, and only when we are willing to surrender can God take control. Confessing our sins to another shows that we are ready to stop running from our pasts and hiding our secrets in the dark. We are ready to get rid of those skeletons in our closets, the same closets where we've been trapped with the enemy who has told us that our sin is too shameful to let it out. It shows our willingness to humble ourselves before God and another human being, bringing reality to our situations.

Confession also shows that we are willing to take action. We're not just thinking or talking about change anymore; we're ready to bear the consequences and take full responsibility for our mistakes or those things that have been holding us captive. We are admitting our need for help. No more excuses, no more denial. We either want change or we just *think* we do—our willingness to confess will be the judge.

Best of all, confession to another opens the door of our hearts to allow what we've been craving all along—unconditional love and acceptance. That night, once I stepped out in faith, I caught my first glimpse of unconditional love, not only from my husband, but, more importantly, from God Himself. God's love was demonstrated to me right in the midst of the most embarrassing, humiliating, painful, and private place in my life. That was His intention. He wanted me to revisit those dark places of my life with Him right beside me so that He could shine a new light on it once and for all.

When Jesus has you address your past, your issues, your wounds, it's not to accuse or torment you. It's not a condemning voice you hear. After the woman admits to Jesus that she doesn't have a husband, He doesn't point His finger at her in shame. He simply says, "You spoke the truth" (John 4:17 MSG).

This is what He wants from us. He wants us to examine ourselves and speak the truth—to ourselves and to Him. The Gospel of John promises that we will know the truth and the *truth* will make us free. We must be willing to see and then admit the truth about our situations. Then we must come to know the real Truth, which is Jesus. Only He can shine a light on the dark places and fill up those gaping wounds in our hearts that this world's hurts have left behind.

Now, I realize that not everyone will have a loving, godly husband who can handle her confession with the grace that mine did that night, but make no mistake: Everyone can find *someone* whom she can reach out to for help. If it's not a spouse, perhaps it's a parent, a trusted friend, or even an unbiased Christian counselor, pastor, or ministry worker. Everyone can find someone to open up to. You're only as alone in life as you choose to be, so reach out! You are not alone. Pray about it. Ask God whom you can trust. He will lead you to a friend who can walk this journey with you and Him. Sometimes that person is the one who can see your pain and is offering their ear to listen, just as Tan-ji was trying to do for me that morning in the hallway at Disney.

Trust God's Word. Confession will ultimately bring healing, not embarrassment (see Jer. 33:6).

Just as I did with Anthony that night, just as the woman at the well did with Jesus, just as Aaron, David, Esther, and Ruth did in all of their biblical greatness, you, too, must face your issues, allowing God to go back with you, before you can ever hope to finally move forward.

Regardless of the source of the pain or the inflictor of the wound, the solution is the same. We must *go*—go back and deal with it once and for all.

Denying it will not change it; we've tried that and it doesn't work. Marrying it away won't fix it (trust me). Eating it away only packs on more problems. Bandaging it with substance abuse, compulsive shopping, and other addictive behaviors haven't worked either.

There is only one solution. And it's not a suggestion; it's a command: Confess it so that you may be healed.

Let's take that first step together.

PEEL BACK THE BANDAGE…

If we're going to administer proper care to this wound, we're going to have to uncover it and have the courage to look at it. Realize, now, that it's not going to be pretty. It will probably be scary at first. But if your desire for change outweighs your desire for comfort, then you must not look away. You must see it—your sin…your offense…your divorce…your abortion…your affair…your abuse. It happened. It's yours. You have to take ownership. It's no one's stumbling block but your own. And it must be *dealt* with, not just *coped* with.

Take heart, this issue may be your stumbling block now. But once you acknowledge its existence and admit your need for healing, it can be used as a stepping-stone out of where you are now and into where God has ordained you to be!

I certainly can vouch for God's ability to turn stumbling blocks into stepping stones. Years after that moment with Anthony when I received healing over my sordid past, God required me to go back yet again to address some other huge, gaping wounds from my past and to remove a major stumbling block from my pathway that had been there for years—the stumbling block of bitterness and hatred towards women! (Yup, you read me correctly!) If you recall, I stated back in Chapter 2 that in high school, after years of mistreatment from girls, I swore off all female relationships—well, in all honesty, it was quite a bit more than that! If I'm being completely transparent with you, I grew to absolutely despise women altogether! Please understand that it wasn't intentional—no sin ever really is. Without even realizing it, I had stored up all of that pain, hurt, and rejection inside of my heart until it later grew into a monster of resentment, distrust, and anger towards women in my adult years—something that God would not allow to remain when He called me into (of all things) women's and girls' ministry! Ultimately, (and trust me when I say it's quite a touching story that neither space nor word count will allow me to tell), God delivered me from all of that pent-up anger and rejection. How, you ask? By giving me a girl of my own—a daughter named Jordan who, only after my receiving an enormous wake-up call and a timely rebuke from a pastor's wife, helped me to heal from the inside out, caused me to love and appreciate women of all ages, and "crossed me over" into my divine purpose in life—to help women find healing and hope from the pain and shame of their pasts!

You see, I would not be where I am today, walking in the fullness and fulfillment of my calling in Christ had I not allowed God (and my Jordan) to bring me back so that He could launch me forward into my appointed destiny!

Are you also ready to step up to your divine purpose? Do you want to see the dreams that God Himself has imagined for you? Then it's time.

GO!

Choose now to go back to discover those tender places from your past before trying to move one more step forward. Because every painful place bears the roots of every ill feeling you have toward God, yourself, and others, this healing is essential to moving forward toward a healthier, happier life. It is the only way.

Now go, rip off that bandage, expose those old, festering, gaping wounds, and trust God to be your Healer. Look at them. Acknowledge them. They are there. We can't change that. But you can lift them up to be healed once and for all. You are not alone. Invite Jesus to go back with you into that painful time of your life. He will. And He will bring with Him all you need to be healed and restored. Now go. Your freedom and your complete healing are waiting.

Acknowledge It

1. Can you identify an event(s) in your past that has kept you from moving forward? What is it? How does it affect you?

2. Can you identify whether or not that event (or events) from your past may have convinced you of the enemy's lies that we identified from chapter 2? What emotions or current beliefs about yourself or God are tied to those events from your past? (We will deal further with these in the coming two chapters, but it's important to identify them now.)

3. Are you willing to do what it takes to go back and confront the issue so that you can be healed? If so, move on to the next question. But if not, what is stopping you?
4. Who in your life can you trust to go back with you for support and accountability?
5. What are some of the feelings you encounter when you think of going back? If they're negative, bring them to God. He understands! What are the positive feelings you experience with the thought of dealing with this once and for all?

Bring It to God

Lord, thank You for caring so much for me that You came along to slice open a tender place so that I may heal once and for all. I admit—I cannot live like this anymore. I want to be healed! I know that You, Lord, can heal me completely from the inside out. I also know that this is not going to be easy, but I am not alone. Help me to trust this process—help me to keep my eyes upon You! You've given me the courage to see those places that need healing, and now, Lord, help me to admit it to another. Show me who I can trust to share my pain with, someone who will go back with me as support and accountability. I trust You. Heal me, God, once and for all, so I can live…for You!

Confess It

I will allow God to heal the tender places in my life.

I am so ready. I can't deny it anymore. I can't cover it up. I can live with my old self no longer, and no longer will I allow my past to hold me back from God's purpose.

I am now willing to face the consequences of wounds that I have inflicted and wounds that have been inflicted upon me.

In order to heal completely, I know that I have to slice them open to the core. I know I must confess everything so that I may be healed.

At this moment, I vow to find someone to share my pain with, someone who will listen to my past and love me in spite of it.

I trust God's promise that I will find perfect healing through confession.

I am ripping off the bandage, and it won't be pretty. But I find comfort in knowing that God is here with me, staring at that same ugly wound—and He loves me anyway. In fact, He's willing to wrap it up in His love and grace and heal it from the inside out.

I am ready. He is waiting. Here I go…

Who ever asked you to feel?
You were chosen to be a princess!
Now go…
Wash your face…
Get a new attitude…
Put on your clothes…
And go be Cinderella!

CHAPTER 5

"Wash Your Face"

PRINCESS PRINCIPLE #4:
MOURN OVER YOUR PAST ONE LAST TIME.

---

*To every thing there is a season, and a time to
every purpose under the heaven…
A time to weep, and a time to laugh; a time to
mourn, and a time to dance.*
~ ECCLESIASTES 3:1, 4 KJV

Once I had escaped Tan-ji and reached the restroom, I could finally
drop the phony smile I had pasted on my face. Glancing up over the
wardrobe counter, I noticed the time: twenty-two minutes until
show time.

Squatting down to look under the stalls, I sighed with relief
upon finding I had the room to myself. As I straightened up and
moved toward the mirror, I caught my reflection and immediately
began sobbing uncontrollably. Unable to catch my breath, I folded

over the basin allowing my tears to fall directly into the sink. Resting my throbbing head on my arm, I mentally checked off all the hurts and offenses I had experienced, crying over each and every one of them. This outpouring of emotion was long overdue.

For several minutes, I held nothing back—I just let it all out. Everything I had bottled up came gushing out of me, until eventually there was nothing left to cry about. Slowly lifting my head, I stared hard at my reflection in the mirror as I ran cold water into my cupped hands below.

The cold, fresh water overflowing out of my hands and down the drain somehow soothed me, bringing warmth and hope to my heart; everything was going to be all right. Inhaling deeply, I bent over the sink once more, this time splashing the water onto my splotched face, hoping to remove any evidence of tears and all signs of grief.

Realizing the time, I quickly dried my face with my towel, slipped out of my sweatpants and into my Cinderella bloomers, and collected my things. Taking a deep breath, I squared my shoulders, released the air from my lungs, and forced a half-cocked smile. It was time to get back to work.

For me, it was several minutes facedown in a cold, porcelain sink. And, years later, it was oceans of tears in my husband's arms. For you, it may have been hours of pillow-soaking sobs. For others, it will be days of silence or solitude. But all of these sad rituals have something in common: They're an important part of the healing process, a process that we call *grieving* or *mourning*.

After the wounds are sliced open and bandages come off, proper healing must follow. As Paula White explains in her book *Deal with It!: You Cannot Conquer What You Will Not Confront*, each wound we experience is an *event*, but healing that wound is a *process*. White goes on to explain that many may mistake *healing* for *forgetting*. But we may *never* forget the event that wounded us. Healing is simply getting beyond the hurting. It is moving into a place where the hurting ceases and we are free from the feelings that go along with that wound.[1]

Grieving or mourning is that God-given process that allows true healing to occur. Mourning isn't just over the death of a loved one. The word *mourn* means to grieve or express sorrow.[2] Any time we experience loss or setback in any form, we experience a reaction to the situation by mourning or expressing our grief. There are many instances in life that can cause us to grieve or express sorrow. It may be the loss of a loved one, a job, or the trust of a friend; a dream that was shattered; a relationship that ended; rejection from another individual; or the failure of a business. Our past or current participation in sin can cause us to grieve as well. When we choose to partake in sin and then come to recognize our failure, we may experience these same stages of grief over our failure.

It should come as no surprise that sin grieves God too. Ephesians 4:30 asks us not to "grieve" the Holy Spirit by the way we live. And, if we are open to hearing the voice of God in the form of conviction, then we, too, will be grieved by our sin and mourn over it.

You have to recognize that your past is a part of your life that will never go away. When it's finally put out in the open, you—along with anyone you've shared it with—have to come to terms with it. It's only then that you can begin sifting through all the emotions and feelings associated with those wounds. An acceptance of your past will come, but not right away.

At the other side of this pain, we can say, "Yes, that event happened, but it does not define me, nor does it hurt to talk about anymore. I have accepted it, and I am stronger for it." But we must not stop short. We come to this only by choosing to walk out all the stages of grief as they come, completely, step-by-step. We must also allow God to be right there with us, leading us through, as we surrender to each stage and then surrender it to God.

> *A time to weep, and a time to laugh; a time to*
> *mourn, and a time to dance.*
> ~ ECCLESIASTES 3:4 KJV

I know you've seen this verse of Scripture—probably numerous times. And if not, you've at least heard it in a Beatles song, right? But the original author of this passage is God, and He wants us to understand that there is a season for everything—even grief.

Note also, however, that there is a time for mourning *and* a time for dancing and that you must have the one before the other can ensue. Perhaps listing them in that order was God's promise to us that when we first mourn properly over our painful losses, we can then be assured that dancing will follow. It's important to also understand that we are supposed to be going *through* the grieving process, not camping out in it. We are certainly not intended to live there. God even put a time limit on the mourning time for the children of Israel when their leader Moses died. After thirty days, it was ended. God told them it was time to get up and move on.

So be encouraged; this time of mourning over your past pain will not last forever. Only you and God can determine how long this process will take.

We find several other examples in the Word of God where it was necessary for individuals to grieve properly before they could move on and embrace their destiny. In the cases of David, Aaron, Esther, and Ruth, they all had to grieve before stepping into the purpose

God had planned for them. In the cases of David and Aaron, their grief was caused by their own choices, while the grief of Esther and Ruth was brought about by circumstances over which they had very little control. Still, all had to deal with their own choices and situations before they could step into their God-given roles.

And thousands of years later, that process is still playing out. God has called imperfect people to serve Him and be examples for Him on this earth, but we must first walk through this healing process—a process that renders a strengthened and healthy mind, body, and spirit—in order for greatness to occur. When this process is completed properly, in spite of any mistakes we've made or any injustices that have been delivered in our lives, we will see God work greatness in our own lives.

So, if this process has been going on for thousands of years, *and* we know that greatness waits just on the other side...why does it always seem so difficult?

The Five Stages of Grief

Well, right now, we're going to break down this process once and for all. We'll explore both the theoretical steps of grief as well as the practical way to walk through it, wash our faces, and live the lives to which Christ has called us.

There are several stages of grief. Some therapists and Christian counselors believe there are as many as ten (which may explain why we sometimes have difficulty understanding the process!). But I want to share with you the five common stages that I have found to be most helpful.

FIVE STAGES OF GRIEF
Denial (Disbelief)
Anger (Turned Outward)
Guilt (Anger Turned Inward[3])
Genuine Grief (Weeping)
Resolution (Acceptance)

Keep in mind as you go that grief doesn't follow a perfect path. Mourning is rarely tidy and is often tumultuous. While you may experience each stage step-by-step in its listed order, the journey is more likely to be a rocky adventure with a combination of stages and emotions coming at you all at once. Either way, for the process to be effective, healing is a journey that cannot be skipped through or shortened. It must be completed in its entirety.

The harmful effects of grieving improperly are both common and widespread. Over the past thirteen years, as an evangelist and a secular motivational speaker throughout the United States and Canada, I have ministered to innumerable women who are stuck in the process. Some are still in denial of their past abuse or sin, while others have gotten beyond the denial stage, but now are stranded in the anger stage—mad at the world, miserable, and making everyone else in their lives miserable too. Or if they are in sin, perhaps they are not denying it, but they are trapped in the *shameful, guilty* stage where they feel like God cannot use them any longer. They cannot move beyond their mistakes.

I've met many women who are still in the weeping stage and still emotionally tender and vulnerable to breaking down. But they never dig down to the root of the problem because they're afraid the floodgates of tears won't stop once they're opened. As a result, they are secretly broken and hurting—privately feeling that they are alone in their struggle and not able to trust anyone with their weaknesses, shame, or reality.

Most women stuck in the grieving process feel like they have to remain strong for those who are depending on them or who look up to them. (I certainly know that feeling, don't you?) So, when they come in contact with pain and loss, they often feel they're "not allowed" to grieve properly. They fear that someone might think them less spiritual if they have a moment of weakness or if they have stumbled into sin.

I must say, this is where I believe that we, as the church, have failed miserably. We, more than anyone, should be able to go to someone the very moment we feel we are beginning to stumble. We should be able to reach out for help *before* we find we have fallen completely into sin! Christians in this predicament often find themselves unable to recoup from their failure because they have no one to confess their sin to in order to be healed. But I digress.

> Unresolved grieving could lead a person into depression.

The saddest thing of all is that unresolved grieving could lead a person into a state of depression. This is a trick of the enemy, to get us trapped in the misery of our past so that it can never become our ministry for the Lord. God intends us to *go through* the process of grieving and washing ourselves of our past pain. Matthew 5:4 says that we are blessed when we mourn because we *will* be comforted. Only after we mourn and receive comfort from the Lord can our pain be turned to purpose, our miseries transformed into powerful ministries. Only then can we extend the very grace that was extended to us in our time of need and hope to a world that is hurting as we once were (see 2 Cor. 1:3–4).

FEEL IT. SAY IT. RELEASE IT.

But if we're grieving, the last thing we're thinking of is how to do it properly, right? Well, as you read about the process, remember that it's a balance. While it's important not to get stuck in a particular phase, it's also just as important to allow each phase to run its course. I believe the most effective way to do this is to allow yourself to *feel* each stage, accepting (not avoiding) whatever emotions it brings; to *say* (or confess) those feelings aloud to God, to yourself, and to another person who can be trusted, acknowledging the feelings' existence; and finally to *release* the emotions properly so as not to hurt yourself or others further, turning them completely over to God.

This walk won't be easy, but you don't have to do it alone. You were never alone. Jesus was there—in the very place your offense took place. He was there when you fell in your sin. He was there when you were abused. He was there when you were victimized and it grieved Him very deeply.

Please hear me when I say that just because God was aware of the event doesn't mean it was His will. God does not put devastating events directly upon us, nor is it ever His will that we are hurt or harmed in any way. The abuse you suffered was not His will; it was your offender's choice to use his or her free will to hurt you. Or it was your choice to enter into sin. But regardless of our paths into the pain, there is always a path out—and a heavenly hand to hold as we walk it.

Shall we?

Stage 1: Denial (Disbelief)

We are in a stage of denial when we refuse to acknowledge and admit what has happened to us and the reality of the situation. Denial is our instinctive protection against the agony of the circumstance. By ignoring its occurrence in our lives, we block out or even escape what we are fearful of accepting. In denial, we often escape into addictive behaviors, withdraw from meaningful relationships, keep ourselves excessively "busy", and even manufacture drama in our lives to keep us distracted from reality.

I've already personally demonstrated several examples of denial, haven't I? Biting my lip, telling Tan-ji and Tommy, "I'm fine," portraying the perfect wife while hiding my past—these are all ways that denial can manifest itself. Can you point to similar instances in your own life?

For many of you, some of these probably came to light as you chose to go back and examine our past in the last chapter. If so, congratulations! You've already got one big step behind you in this process. (See, that was easy!)

If you're still dealing with denial on unresolved issues, that's okay too. But know that in order to move *through* this stage, you must stop looking away, take ownership, and deal with the offense as a reality that will not go away. Proverbs 28:13 tells us that he who covers his sins will not prosper, but whoever *confesses* and *forsakes* them will have mercy.

We escape into addictive behaviors to keep us distracted from reality.

I know you're ready for mercy. It's waiting.

Start by talking to God. Pray. God is already aware of the sin or offense against you. He is already aware of the shame that you feel.

He is already aware of the huge, gaping hole you've been trying to fill with other things besides Him. Ignoring it or denying it only prolongs the healing. So just tell Him. Tell Him how you feel about it. He cares. Hebrews 4:15–16 tells us that Jesus understands our weaknesses and issues, and we can go to His throne and receive grace and mercy in our time of need. Remember that your stumbling blocks can be changed into stepping-stones if you'll turn them over to God.

Once we admit it to Him, He is faithful to remove it from us (see 1 John 1:9). King David said it like this: "Finally, I confessed all my sins to you and stopped trying to hide my guilt. I said to myself, 'I will confess my rebellion to the LORD.' And you forgave me! All my guilt is gone" (Ps. 32:5 NLT).

As you remember the event, try to recall every last detail. Go back to that place and think on it. Feel it. Say it. And release what you feel as it comes—don't hold it in! It's important that it becomes real to you again—not because God wants to hurt you, but because He wants you to let Him into that painful place and allow His healing to take place.

Many people are in denial because they don't want to remember the pain or experience the emotions that accompanied the event. They fear it's just too much for them to bear. If this is the case for you, friend, then let me suggest that, in addition to Jesus, you should find someone who can walk this journey with you, such as a Christian psychologist or certified counselor, or even simply a trusted adult friend. Depending on your experience, professional help may be critical for your healing. Don't allow fear to keep you from your freedom.

Stage 2: Anger (Turned Outward)

In this stage, we are simply angry that this event has happened to us. We feel rage and anger that this situation has interrupted our lives and changed everything. Often during this stage, logic and reason are irrelevant. Anger can usually be accompanied by the feeling of being out of control. Plus, if anger is directed toward a loved one or to God, this can lead to feelings of guilt. For many people, anger can be the most disconcerting of the stages of grief.

To most effectively deal with our anger in this stage, we first must determine with whom we are angry, and if our anger is appropriate or inappropriate. And above all, we must be honest with ourselves.

Perhaps your anger is directed at your abuser, or the person who betrayed or abandoned you, or toward the person who participated in sin with you. The difficult thing here is that we often feel justified in our anger. We were betrayed...hurt...abandoned...misled.

Understand that anger has a place. Jesus was angry in the temple and overturned the tables. His anger was a response to barricades that were blocking God's salvation from reaching human lives. It was not a reaction to being threatened. His divine sense of justice was offended. His anger was kindled.

Psychiatrists Minirth and Meier explain, "Some of our anger is quite an appropriate response...to someone who has sinned against us."[4] This would include someone truly treating you unjustly or unfairly—a "friend" lying about you or spreading rumors, or someone who took advantage of you or abused you as a child.

Whatever the case may be, the Bible never instructs us not to get angry, it merely instructs us not to remain angry: "Go ahead and be angry. You do well to be angry—but don't use your anger as fuel for revenge. And don't stay angry. Don't go to bed angry. Don't give the Devil that kind of foothold in your life" (Eph. 4:26–27 MSG). I think it's important to point out that while we often cite Ephesians 4:26 to instruct married couples not to go to bed angry at each other, there's a far greater implication here that relates to each and every one of us—married or not.

We are instructed to deal responsibly with our anger and negative emotions (i.e. frustration, fear, and sadness) by bedtime because when these emotions are internalized, they contribute to an over-utilization of the serotonin and norepinephrine in the brain (often caused by lack of restful sleep due to our inner turmoil). And "the net result of mental depression is physical depression, which in turn contributes to the development of physical illnesses..."[5] In other words, God is saying: Do your spirit, soul, and body a favor—deal with your emotions properly and promptly!

Often when we go through something traumatic, we may also become angry with God for not stopping it. However, anger toward God is inappropriate. According to Psalm 103, God is righteous, fair, and loving. Romans 8:28 tells us that "in all things God works for the good of those who love him."

Even without Scripture, anger toward God is an emotion that we, as God's children, know almost instinctively to be wrong. For that reason, when we're angry with God, we're not only dealing with anger, we're also dealing with *denial* of being angry with God or with *guilt* over being angry with God.

Admitting our feelings of anger is key. Even if we are angry with God, we must tell Him. If you are angry with someone else, confess this also to God. *He* already knows how you are feeling, but again, this makes *us* aware of the truth.

In *Happiness Is a Choice*, Minirth and Meier hold fast to their conviction that the root problem in nearly all depressions is pent-up anger and holding grudges against self, others, or God.[6] As such, they recommend that anger should ideally be ventilated both to God (vertically) and to men (horizontally). If we are convinced that our anger is appropriate, then in accordance with Matthew

> *Release your emotions daily.*

5:21–24 and Ephesians 4:26, we are instructed to go to the person who has offended us and talk to him or her about it. This act of obedience takes a great deal of courage and maturity. Please make sure that when you go to the person you are angry with that you are able to do so in love and in control of your emotions. Pray about it, asking God to give you wisdom. For instance, if you were abused thirty years ago as a child by a relative who is now deceased, it would not be wise to go to their next of kin or spouse and reveal it to them after all those years. That would only bring pain and hurt to that family member and friction among the family. Going to a trusted adult or counselor to share this offense would be wiser. Use wisdom. If God does have you go to your offender, know that this can be a real challenge, especially if the person has truly violated, abused, or betrayed you. And be prepared that you may not always receive the response you are hoping for. Nevertheless, do what God would have you to do and then determine to leave the rest to Him.

The human response to being harmed by someone else is to seek retribution to make him or her pay for what he or she has done. However, here's what the apostle Paul says about vengeance: "Never pay back evil with more evil....Dear friends, never take revenge. Leave that to the righteous anger of God" (Rom. 12:17, 19 NLT). Let God be the avenger for the wrong done against you.

Confessing your anger is so that you can be free and move on. It's not a tool to harm the person you are angry with, no matter how justified you may feel you would be in doing so. Walking around angry all of the time is destructive and can lead to depression.

Once you've confessed your anger, focus on finding a constructive way of venting it. You may need to experiment with several different activities before you find the one that works for you. Taking a jog or a long walk can be very therapeutic. A friend of mine in ministry was left with a lot of built-up anger after a very traumatic time in her marriage. When she felt herself becoming angry or anxious, she simply took a walk. Around and around her neighborhood she walked, releasing the anger with each step. I have another friend who boxes. She literally has a rubber man in her garage and she puts on boxing gloves and punches the daylights out of him. Some also find writing their feelings down is very helpful. Even though the journal is kept private, just the act of putting emotions into words on paper is an effective way to vent. Try one of these or find another similar, constructive means for venting your anger. The goal is to release your emotions daily in order to prevent them from building up and kindling anger within you. Remember, anger that is repressed can lead to depression so be sure to deal with it properly and promptly!

Stage 3: Guilt (Anger Turned Inward)

Notice that we're calling guilt "anger turned inward." That is because guilt is a form of pent-up anger and must be dealt with accordingly. As Minirth and Meier point out, "guilt is anger toward yourself." As the focus turns inward, there's an impulse to blame or hold yourself responsible whether you are (true guilt) or not (false guilt). A common feeling is, "Someone should have to pay for this!" And you take it on yourself. You feel that you could have taken proper action to prevent the circumstances or situation. You feel shame or embarrassment.

The guilt felt in this stage is comprised of true guilt, false guilt, or a combination of both. *False guilt* is when we blame or hold ourselves responsible for something we truly had no control over, such as being sexually molested as a child. A child who is hurt by an adult or another person in such a manner is *never* responsible. The offender is fully responsible and to blame for his or her own actions.

There are many other instances of abuse, neglect, or trauma that have been suffered at the hands of someone else. You must examine your heart and mind and determine if you've been blaming yourself for something that was out of your control.

True guilt, on the other hand, is the emotion we experience when we actually were in the wrong. The offense occurred as a result of our choices or actions. Perhaps it was an affair, an abortion, a crime, or any number of other sins we are feeling guilty over. This is something we *should* feel when we've sinned. Earlier we mentioned Aaron's and David's grief over sins they'd committed. This guilt or shame is a result of the conviction of the Holy Spirit. We shouldn't harden our hearts against this conviction but rather be open to His instruction and correction. But you must understand the difference here: *Conviction* comes from the Holy Spirit as correction or warning to your conscience. *Condemnation* comes from the enemy as an attempt to harass you and keep you beat down over your sin even after you've asked for forgiveness.

Choose to accept His payment for your sins.

Once you've made a determination of true guilt or false guilt, confess it. Tell Jesus about it. If you're feeling ashamed over something that was done to you, confess it to your Savior and ask Him to take away your guilt and shame. *It's not yours to carry.* Remember, we are told in the book of Isaiah that Christ bore our shame and sorrow. He carried it to the cross with Him; don't let that be in vain. Choose to accept His payment for your sins. If you're feeling guilty over your own sin, confess it and ask God to forgive you. He will (see 1 John 1:9).

One of the most beautiful psalms is Psalm 51. David wrote it after confessing His sin with Bathsheba to God. He asked the Lord to have mercy on him, cleanse him, purify his heart, and restore the joy of salvation. And God did.

He wants to do the same for you. Release it; let it go! If you've asked God to take your guilt and shame, that's exactly what He has done. Thank God for His forgiveness and don't allow your feelings to tell you any different. It's done. "Those who look to him for help will be radiant with joy; no shadow of shame will darken their faces" (Ps. 34:5 NLT). He said He would forgive us if we would ask, and He has.

A good friend, Jessie Rogers Goodman, wrote and sings a song, "Come to Me," that has ministered to hurting souls across the nation. It is based upon a promise by Jesus found in Matthew 11:28: "Come to me, all you who are weary and burdened, and I will give you rest." If you're weary from carrying the burden of guilt and shame, then after you feel it and say it, release it in a healthy manner—Jesus wants you to have rest!

Stage 4: Genuine Grief (Weeping)

This is the stage where we let it all out. Weep. Mourn. Wail. It's our physical release of emotional angst or pain that allows us to release what has been bottled up for so long. This is a necessary stage that many people, even a lot of Christians, never allow themselves to experience for fear of "losing it." But allowing yourself to feel every last bit of anguish is necessary to get to the next and final stage of this grieving process.

You're not alone in your grief. As evidenced in the following chart, there are many references in the Bible to grieving or mourning. Throughout, mourning was expressed by weeping or loud lamentation. So go ahead and weep. It's a perfectly natural response to emotional pain.

MOURNING FOR THE DEAD	
Abraham for Sarah	Genesis 23:2
Jacob for Joseph	Genesis 37:34–35
Egyptians for Jacob	Genesis 50:3–10
Israel for Aaron	Numbers 20:29
For Moses	Deuteronomy 34:8
For Samuel	1 Samuel 25:1
David for Abner	2 Samuel 3:31-35
Mary and Martha for Lazarus	John 11
Men for Stephen	Acts 8:2

MOURNING OVER CALAMATIES OR TRAGEDY	
Job	Job 1:20–21; 2:8
Israel	Exodus 33:4
The Ninevites	Jonah 3:5
Israel	Judges 20:26

Whether your tears are a result of what's been done to you or a sin you've committed, there is Someone you can turn to and trust with your grief: Jesus. He fully understands what you are feeling. Isaiah 53:3–6 (NLT) says:

> He [Jesus] was despised and rejected—a man of sorrows, acquainted with deepest grief. We turned our backs on him and looked the other way. He was despised, and we did not care. Yet it was our weaknesses he carried; it was our sorrows that weighed him down. And we thought his troubles were a punishment from God, a punishment for his own sins! But he was pierced for our rebellion, crushed for our sins. He was beaten so

we could be whole. He was whipped so we could be healed. All of us, like sheep, have strayed away. We have left God's paths to follow our own. Yet the LORD laid on him the sins of us all.

Just like us, Jesus experienced sorrow. He knew what it was to feel forsaken (see Mark 15:34). He knew what it was to grieve. He knows what you are feeling. The Scripture says that it was our sorrows and pain that weighed Him down. You can cry all of your anguish out to Him. He understands.

Release it now to Him. You, too, can then proclaim as the psalmist did, "You have turned my mourning into joyful dancing. You have taken away my clothes of mourning and clothed me with joy" (Ps. 30:11 NLT).

Stage 5: Resolution (Acceptance)

In this stage, you determine to move on. But this stage occurs only once you have worked through the stages of denial, anger, guilt, and genuine grief. *Acceptance* is what we often term as "closure," and it is a good thing! You *resolve* yourself to continuing your life *in spite of* the circumstances or tragedy you have faced or endured. Resolution or the resolve to move forward is where the hurt stops and the healing is complete, leaving only a scar that can now tell a wonderful story of God's healing grace!

To fully release our grief and move forward with resolution, we must finally embrace forgiveness. We must first receive forgiveness from God. Then we must choose to forgive our offenders, as well as ourselves.

1. **Choose to accept freely God's forgiveness as He freely gave it.**
   No matter what the offense, God loves you! Romans 3: 23–24 says, "For everyone has sinned; we all fall short of

God's glorious standard. Yet God, with undeserved kindness, declares that we are righteous. He did this through Christ Jesus when He freed us from the penalty for our sins" (NLT). Accept this forgiveness, declaring it through prayer: *I freely accept God's forgiveness. I am forgiven because God's Word says that when I have sinned I can come boldly to the throne of grace where I can ask for forgiveness and it shall be done. It is nothing I have earned or deserve, but it is a free gift from God.*

No matter what the offense, God loves you!

Remind yourself now, that not only has God forgiven you but He has forgotten it (see Jer. 31:34). Don't go dragging it back up to God again in prayer, because He has already forgotten it. And so should you!

2. **Choose to forgive your offender.**

   Let me point out here, forgiving your offender is a free will, conscious choice. You do this based on a decision, not a feeling, to forgive. Unforgiveness held in your heart toward your offender is not hurting anyone but yourself. This fear-based emotion is toxic to your thought life and to your body. So just do it. Choose to leave your offender in God's hands. Choose to free yourself. Choose to forgive. Then once you do, start by trying to empathize with your offender. Perhaps your offender hurt you because he himself is a hurting person. As the saying goes, "Hurting people hurt people." Perhaps empathizing with him will shed some light on his or her own need for forgiveness. This is difficult, but it is possible with God's power. The person who hurt you may deserve for you to be angry with him, but you are choosing to forgive instead.

Forgiveness is a choice based on God's forgiveness for you through the death of His Son on the cross. If we expect forgiveness, we must demonstrate forgiveness. In fact, Jesus states, "For if you forgive men when they sin against you, your heavenly Father will also forgive you. But if you do not forgive men their sins, your Father will not forgive your sins" (Matt. 6:14–15).

Jesus was our ultimate example of forgiveness. While He was nailed to the cross, bleeding, and in excruciating pain from the horrendous beating He'd just suffered, He prayed for forgiveness for His accusers and tormentors. If Jesus can do it, He can give us the strength to do it too. Ask Him to place forgiveness inside of your heart. And then, whether your flesh and emotions *feel* like it or not, forgive by faith. Ask God's help with this *daily* until your emotions align with your forgiveness in faith. It may not happen instantly or even quickly, but it will happen as you daily choose to forgive.

3. **Choose to forgive yourself.**

This is often the hardest and most neglected part but ever so vital to your future! Choosing not to forgive yourself will only result in your continuing to walk through life as a hurting person who hurts others and is easily hurt and offended by the actions of others. (And you don't want that!) The Word tells us that we are a *new creation* in Christ. You have to choose to let go of the things in your past. Choose not to dwell on the things you did; choose to forgive yourself. What you did and who you are in Christ are two totally separate things. When you have the urge to torment, punish, or condemn yourself for your past sins, *stop!* Stop and remind yourself that those things are under the blood of Jesus. It's been paid for. Leave it there! Know that once God forgives you of it, He remembers it no more. Do not feel the need to relive it, repent of it again, or rehearse it to God; He has forgiven it and forgotten it!

> ### Those who stare at the past
> ### have their backs turned to the future.[7]

Forgiveness is often misunderstood as excusing or minimizing the offense. As with the woman caught in the act of adultery brought before Jesus to be stoned, Jesus acknowledged her sin by saying, "Go and sin no more" (John 8:11 NKJV). He didn't dwell on it—He didn't have to. She was fully aware of what she had done. Forgiveness can also be misunderstood as an attempt to deny or avoid our pain. However, when done correctly, it does neither.

It is not a choice to forget about what happened, but rather a choice not to dwell on what happened. You may not be able to stop a haunting memory from popping into your head, but you *can* choose not to think on it, because thinking on it would cause you to move into negative beliefs and behaviors. When those thoughts of your abuse or sin begin to plague you, bring it to God. Choose not to dwell on those thoughts. (More on that in the next chapter.)

Once you've asked Jesus to forgive you of your sin, do not allow yourself to take it back from God. "He has removed our sins as far from us as the east is from the west," according to Psalm 103:12 (NLT), and will not remember it again. When the enemy tries to remind you of your past failure or pain, remind him of the day—this day—that you accepted forgiveness or that you declared forgiveness of your offender. (Write the date here in the margin if you need to!) Don't allow yourself to wallow in your past and dwell on what you have already put into the Lord's hands. It's over. It's now time to move on, to *wash your face* of any signs of your former grief.

Remember David and Ruth? Before this man and woman of God could move on and into their destinies, each of them had to get up from where they were, in their loneliness, despair, failure, pain, or sin, and choose to take the first step out of it. The first step they took was the step of washing themselves, or in other words, cleansing themselves.

Following the tragic events involving David's child with Bathsheba, Second Samuel 12:20 says, "Then David got up from the ground. After he had washed, put on lotions and changed his clothes, he went into the house of the LORD and worshiped." (Well, it also says that he ate, but that's only because he's a man. Men can always eat in the midst of any tragedy!) In Ruth 3:3, we read, "Wash and perfume yourself, and put on your best clothes."

They both illustrate perfectly that our situation doesn't have to change in order for us to wash ourselves off and move on. David's son was still dead, as was Ruth's husband. But you've got to wash off yesterday's filth in order to move into the promise of a better tomorrow. Otherwise, we're just taking it with us into our future. You can't go into your tomorrow smelling like yesterday!

Now, put your past in the past and *make it* stay there. Stop rehearsing it and bringing it up over and over again to your girlfriends. Stop talking about it as though it's still a fresh, open wound. Let it heal. Let it scar over. The only way you should be talking about it from here on is as a testimony of God's healing—which is exactly what a scar is, a reminder of where there was once pain, but is no more.

These steps we have just walked are steps that we must learn to do well. We will have to practice them regularly. We're not promised an easy road without sorrows, letdowns, or trials. There is no guarantee that our tomorrow will be any easier than our yesterday. We have come a long way, but make no mistake: As long as we're on this earth, we will have struggles with sin and temptation. We will have others who cause injury and an enemy who is constantly seeking to devour us. We will experience loss, disappointments, and heartaches. Therefore, learning how to look these things in the eye, grieve over them properly, and release them to the Lord is crucial both now and for the rest of our lives. Although there are no guarantees that we will never again suffer loss, we now know how to properly heal our wounds. And, as we have witnessed throughout this process together, we also have a guarantee that we will never be alone through any of it (see Heb. 13:5).

You have chosen well. You chose to mourn one last time, and you have chosen to let it go. Now give yourself permission to do as David did. Get up and wash your face. God has great plans for your life. It's time to get back to what you were called to do.

Acknowledge It

1. Has God revealed some events in your life that were not mourned over properly? What are they? Have you taken the steps to do so?
2. By reading this chapter, have you discovered that you are "stuck" in the grieving process? What stage would you say you are stuck in? Denial? Anger? Guilt? Weeping? Or can you say you have now come to resolution? Explain.
3. How are you doing in the forgiveness category? Are you harboring any unforgiveness in your heart toward anyone?

Have you forgiven yourself, or are you carrying around guilt or shame from an event that God already forgave? Are you at complete peace with God for the trials He allowed you to walk through?

4. Have you washed your face, ready to move on to all that God has in store for you? What are some of His promises you expect to see come to fruition in your life?

BRING IT TO GOD

Lord, You see where I have been and where I am now. None of it surprises You. In fact, now I know that You've just been waiting for me to bring it to You. Because I trust You, I give You permission to examine my heart. Help me to be honest about my past and how it has affected me. Help me to walk through these stages of grief one by one, as painful as they might be. Be with me as I see, feel, admit, and release the offenses once and for all. Give me the courage and the strength not to turn back. Please, God, cast out all of my fears by Your perfect love! And help me to accept Your forgiveness unconditionally. Please, Lord, place forgiveness in my heart daily so I can extend it to my offenders. This I cannot do on my own, but with You, I know it is possible. Thank You for setting me free, day by day, step by step, through this process of healing.

CONFESS IT

I will mourn over my past one last time.

My life has not been one of perfection. I have deep wounds that have gone untouched and unhealed for far too long. That ends today.

I have begun to move through the grieving process and am allowing myself to walk through each step, feeling it completely, confessing it, and releasing it—never to harm me again—into the open arms of God.

Once released, the healing is complete. I have accepted my past and will only speak of it in testimony to God's amazing grace.

I will wash my face and arise a woman ready for the divine purposes that God has set before me.

Ecclesiastes 3:4 tells me that there is a time to mourn and a time to dance.

I am ready to dance.

Who ever asked you to feel?

You were chosen to be a princess!

Now go...

Wash your face...

Get a new attitude...

Put on your clothes...

And go be Cinderella!

CHAPTER 6

"Get a New Attitude"

PRINCESS PRINCIPLE #5:
FORM A NEW ATTITUDE BASED
ON THE TRUTHS OF GOD.

And do not be conformed to this world,
but be transformed by the renewing of
your mind.

~ ROMANS 12:2 NASB

After squaring my shoulders and resolving to get back to work, I stood for another moment in front of the mirror, taking one last deep breath. I released the air from my lungs, and in an instant it felt as though a heavy weight had been lifted from my shoulders. Taken aback by my feeling of relief, I thought, *Was that all I needed—a really good cry?*

Leaning into the mirror, I inspected my face a bit closer and then leaned back away. I forced my best smile, but something had changed. This time, the smile came a little easier. Brushing the hair back from my face, I reminded myself of Tommy's last words. "Get a new attitude," he had said.

Yeah…a new attitude. And just how do I do that?

In a moment, I began to reason with myself. *I have no choice. I have to change. I'm not ready to quit. I can do this.*

So, I said those words out loud to myself in the mirror: "You can do this, Jen. You can do this."

The more I spoke those words, the easier they came.

"You can do this. *You* were chosen. You're a princess. You can do this!" Out loud, I repeated those words to myself over and over again.

Then I began to speak them from my heart. "I can do this. I am a princess. I was chosen. I'm a princess."

Before long, the muffled reassurance actually became faith-filled words of purpose that moved me. As I turned toward the door and reached for the handle, I kept repeating that statement to myself: "I can do this. I'm a princess. I can do this. I *am* a princess."

Weakness of attitude becomes weakness
of character.

~ Albert Einstein

I know you've heard, "Attitude is everything." But have you ever looked up the word *attitude* to see what it really means? I did. And it gave me a much clearer picture of how our attitudes can affect everything else in our lives.

I've learned that when Tommy told me to get a new attitude, he wasn't just telling me to change my mood; he was instructing me to get a new outlook, a new mind-set, a new way of thinking and behaving! He was telling me to get a new *perspective*. And that is exactly what I'm encouraging you to get now—a new perspective on your past, on your present, and on your purpose.

> *Get a new perspective on your past, on your present, and on your purpose.*

But perspectives, mind-sets, and attitudes don't change themselves. We must choose to get a new attitude and develop a new mind-set if we are going to enjoy our newfound freedom from those things that we so courageously dealt with and let go of thus far.

There are many cases in the Bible where men and women of God had to do what Tommy instructed me to do—get a new attitude. Only instead of the Bible saying the words, *David got an attitude adjustment* or *Ruth changed her attitude*, it said that they *anointed* themselves. David and Ruth, as we mentioned in the last chapter, washed and anointed themselves and then moved on into the purpose God had for them.

In Bible times, the meaning of anointing someone or something was this:

- To consecrate[1]
- To set apart
- To anoint oneself (with oil or lotions)[2]

The person who was anointed or consecrated unto God was a person who was chosen by God, called out, set apart—one who would walk differently, talk differently, and have a different attitude from the rest. That was David. He was chosen and anointed by God to be king. But he later had an adulterous affair with Bathsheba, a beautiful but married woman. He then had her husband sent to the front lines of the battle where he was killed. After this, David married Bathsheba, and their union produced a son. The Bible says that the things David did displeased the Lord, and the baby became very ill. David grieved, fasted, and prayed to God for the child's recovery. In spite of this, his newborn son died. The servants were afraid to tell David the news of his son's death because of how sorrowful he was during the child's illness. However, David reacted in a way that astounded them.

"Then David *arose* from the earth, and *washed*, and *anointed* himself, and changed his apparel, and came into the house of the Lord, and worshipped: then he came to his own house; and when he required, they set bread before him, and he did eat" (2 Sam.12:20 KJV, emphasis mine).

In this particular verse, the word *anoint* is derived from the Hebrew word *cuwk*, which means to anoint oneself as was customary after bathing (as with lotions). But it seems that for David it was more than just the ritualistic act of applying lotion or oil to make himself smell better. He made a conscious decision to get up, wash, and anoint—or get a new attitude.

Understand that his situation had not changed—his son was still dead. But I believe when David washed and anointed himself after the death of his son, he was remembering when he was first anointed to be king. Studies show that when a person was anointed, there was a distinct aroma that permeated off of them from the oil. It was evident to anyone near them that they'd been anointed. Maybe he was saying to himself as he took the oil, "I was chosen. I'm a king."

Perhaps as he applied the oil onto himself, he spoke those words aloud. Perhaps as the aroma filled the room and he breathed it, he got a new attitude. David had a revelation, one that you and I need to grasp as well: He could not change his circumstance, but he *could* change his attitude!

He could have easily chosen to continue lying on the ground mourning the loss of his son and grieving over his sin. Who could have blamed him? But he did not. Knowing that lying there in his grief would not bring his son back to life, he got up and went on to reign as the anointed king whom God had ordained. And he is now known as a man after God's own heart!

She could have walked around complaining about the unfairness of life. But she chose differently.

Now let's take a look at Ruth. Ruth's husband died, leaving her without children. Afterward, she chose to follow her mother-in-law, Naomi, back to her homeland. In the book of Ruth chapter 2, Ruth is a widow, living in a foreign land, working in the fields of a man named Boaz, a close relative of Naomi. She is working to support and feed her mother-in-law and herself by coming behind the harvesters in the field and gathering their leftover grain.

When Boaz arrives at his field, he spots Ruth and asks his servants who she is. The young men tell him of Ruth and her kindness to her mother-in-law. Boaz is impressed by the young woman's *attitude* and instructs his workers to drop extra grain on purpose so that she is able to gather even more.

In Ruth chapter 3, Naomi tells Ruth she is going to help her find a home (and a husband). In verse three, Naomi tells her daughter-in-law to wash herself, anoint herself (put on some perfume or lotion), get dressed, and go down to the threshing floor where Boaz was. And Ruth answered, "I will do whatever you say" (3:5). And she did.

Her attitude was amazing. Her situation had not changed—she was still a childless widow, still a foreigner. She could have walked around murmuring and complaining to herself about the injustice of it all, at the unfairness of life. But she chose differently.

She washed the filth of the field off her. She washed away her grief. She would not forget the husband whom she loved, but she could not bring him back. She had to go forward, to embrace the plan God had for her. Ruth anointed herself and dressed and went to meet Boaz.

Now she further amazed Boaz, who had already recognized this woman's noble character—so much so that he married her! God blessed Boaz and Ruth with a son.

"And they named him Obed. He became the father of Jesse and the grandfather of David" (Ruth 4:17 NLT).

Recognize that name? Ruth was David's great-grandmother, and later down the line came Jesus Christ! Largely because of her great attitude, God's plan for Ruth was fulfilled.

"Get a new attitude." Your future may depend upon it.

Perspective = Position + Focus

One of the things that God showed me about these great people of the Bible—Esther, Ruth, David, and Aaron—was that they all went through the same process to get to their appointed destinies. They all washed themselves (as we did in the previous chapter), and they all, including Aaron and Esther, anointed themselves. They gained a new mind-set so they could then move forward into their destinies. Or as the Scripture says, they were choosing not to dwell on what lay behind them so that they could focus solely on what was ahead of them (see Phil. 3:13). They knew that the past was in the past, and they must get a new attitude in order to focus properly on their future in Christ. We must learn to do the same.

The only way to fully enjoy the present and properly enter our future is to have an attitude, outlook, and mind-set founded on Truth. We now know that coming into agreement with the lie of the enemy has brought us into sin, shame, trials, misdirected beliefs, and faulty mind-sets (such as the ones listed on your 3 x 5 cards). The only antidote for the enemy's lies is to get into agreement and alignment with the Truth. We do that by choosing to listen and respond only to the voice of God and by changing our perspective to His perspective!

Perspective is always contingent on your position.

What I have come to discover is this: If our perspective is off, then it is entirely because of two things—our position has changed, and our focus is skewed. Let's deal with position first.

POSITIONING YOURSELF FOR PROPER PERSPECTIVE

As you can well imagine, my perspective of life as a Disney Princess changed dramatically once I became one! When I was seven looking at Cinderella in her magical stagecoach and dreaming of the day I would be in her shoes, I was experiencing Disney as a guest in the park standing at ground-level, parade-side, seeing her through starry, seven-year-old eyes that had not yet been exposed to the cruelty and reality of life. I gained a whole new perspective when I was an eighteen-year-old Disney Cast Member with a backstage pass, standing atop a Cinderella parade float, struggling desperately to see anything *but* the realities and pains of this life. My position in life had changed, and because of that I saw things differently.

Perspective is always contingent on your position. In the story of Adam and Eve, once Eve was moved by her emotions and changed her position to side with the enemy, her perspective was also changed. With a change of position, she and Adam came to see God differently, themselves differently, and others differently. Their new perspective caused them to fear and hide from the very God that they had walked with each day. They looked down at themselves and noticed that they were naked as they had always been, except now, they were filled with shame (see Gen. 3:7–10) and ducked into the bushes to cover themselves. They taught us that our position does in fact determine our perspective.

So, in order for our perspectives, our attitudes, and our mindsets to change, we're going to have to change our position by stepping up just a little bit higher.

Perspective answers the why questions of life.

~ Rick Warren[3]

Let's examine where we stand right now. Please take out those 3 x 5 cards that you filled out from chapter 2. On them, you should have your thoughts, feelings, and perceptions of God, yourself, and others.

If you examine them, you will be able to determine where you stand—on the enemy's side with a lie or on God's side with the Truth. And how do you know that? Well, let's take a look at some examples.

Let's take our perception and attitudes toward God. If my 3 x 5 card reads, "I feel like God abandoned me at the time I needed Him the most! He wasn't there for me!" than my attitude toward God would be based on a lie. How do I know that? Because the Truth—the Word of God—in Hebrews 13:5 tells me that God is *always* with me and that He will never leave me nor forsake me. And in

Matthew 28:20, He tells me that He is with me always, even unto the ends of the earth.

That is the Truth—it is God's Word. And since the attitude I have does not align with that Truth, I know that it is founded upon a lie—a lie that the enemy fed me in the hour of my deepest need in order to make me *feel* like God did not care about me. I could have chosen to reject the lie, but I chose rather to believe it and to change my position by standing with the enemy instead of with God. I foolishly based my beliefs about God on the feelings I was experiencing during a moment of despair. The result was a negative attitude toward God, which keeps me distant from Him and His healing love. That's the trick of the enemy, and I fell for it!

When these negative attitudes are formed, it is imperative that we learn how to change that perception and belief about God, because how we view God is so very vital to the relationship we have with Him. A. W. Tozer once wrote in *The Knowledge of the Holy*, "It is impossible to keep our moral practices sound and our inward attitudes right while our idea of God is erroneous or inadequate."[4] He went on to say this:

What I believe about God is the most important thing about me.

Let's say your 3 x 5 card reads: "No one—not even God—will ever be able to forgive me for what I have done. My life is ruined!" However, the Truth of God says in 1 John 1:9 that all we have to do is confess our sins to God, and then He is faithful and just to forgive us of all of our sins and to cleanse us completely. It also says in Jeremiah 29:11 that God knows the plans He has for you. "They are plans for good and not for disaster, to give you a future and a hope" (NLT). And Philippians 1:6 tells you that God has begun a good work in you, and He promises to carry that work out to its completion! If you know the character of God, you know that He is not a God who gives up on us but rather is patient with us (see Ps. 86:15; 2 Pet. 3:9). So again, this attitude you have developed toward yourself and your future is based on a lie that the enemy convinced you of through the feelings and the circumstances of your life.

Do you get my point? It's simple. There is Truth and then there is a lie. If we stand on the lie, our perspective is off. But if we crawl up into God's loving arms and see our world from His perspective, we will see it differently. So let me ask you: Who's voice have you been listening and responding to? Which side have you chosen to stand with? What have you come into agreement with and who have you chosen to believe? God or the enemy?

It's important that you answer that last question, because all behavior is rooted in belief! What you believe in your heart is what has determined your behavior. As the saying goes, where your heart goes, your body eventually follows.

A lie believed as truth will affect you as if it were true.

~ Craig Groeschel

There is no straddling the fence. We either believe God and take Him at His Word, or we reject it (whether purposely or inadvertently) and come into agreement with the enemy's lie. Based on the answers on your 3 x 5 cards, where do you stand? On the Truth or on the lie?

Don't worry. The good news is: If you discover today that you're standing on the wrong side and your behavior and your attitudes are based on faulty mind-sets, then all you have to do is switch sides! Change positions. Line yourself up with God's Truths and watch your perspective begin to change. With the proper perspective, you will begin to see your attitudes come in agreement with your newfound outlook on life, and eventually you'll notice your behaviors will begin to align with your newfound beliefs! (More on exactly *how* to do that in a moment.)

What You Focus on the Longest Becomes Strongest

Now, the other thing that must be examined in order to change our perspective and our attitude is our focus. If our attitude is off, then our focus must be skewed. Let's look at what we've been focused on that might have brought us to where we are right now so we can begin to change our course.

We just discovered which side we've been standing on, and it only stands to reason that if we've been standing with the lie, then we've probably been staring hard at it too. The saying is true that what we choose to focus on the longest will become strongest in our lives.

I have an illustration I do in my conferences that helps us to understand the importance of our focus and just how quickly our focus can be altered. I sit a participant down on a chair and hand her two pieces of paper. One paper says "TRUTH"; the other says "LIE." I ask her to hold the papers side by side so that they are both visible at the same time. Then I ask her to choose one of the papers to focus on intently. She may choose whichever word she desires, spending the next three to four minutes staring hard at that word on the paper. After several minutes, I come back to her and ask her not to look up. As she keeps her focus on her chosen word, I ask her which word she chose to focus on. Most of the time, the participant chose to focus on the word "TRUTH." With that, I then ask her, "What do you see now?"

Almost every time she answers—completely unscripted— something like this: "I see 'TRUTH'—that's all I see. Actually, the 'LIE' is now completely blurry!"

And my point is easily made.

You see, if we choose daily to focus on the Truth of God's Word and His good plan for our lives, then eventually, the lie of the world will fade out or become blurry. And the same is true of the opposite. If we choose to focus heavily on the lie of the world, eventually God's Truth will grow blurry, and we won't be able to see Him or His ways clearly anymore.

Part of our problem is that our focus has been on the wrong thing—the lie—for so long, that we can no longer see the correct thing—the Truth. That must change if we hope to change our ways.

FOCUS ON THE POSITIVE

The Bible does us a huge favor in telling us precisely what we are to focus on. We are told in Philippians 4:8 to focus on "whatsoever things are true, whatsoever things are honest, whatsoever things are just, whatsoever things are pure, whatsoever things are lovely, whatsoever things are of good report; if there be any virtue, and if there be any praise, think on these things" (KJV). In other words, if it lines up with God's Word and it encourages you in your faith and in your heart, then focus on those things. We are not to be focusing on anything that goes against God's Word or choosing to allow any negative, aggravating, demeaning thoughts to infiltrate our thought life. We may not have control over what happens to us

> *If it lines up with God's Word and it encourages you in your faith, then focus on those things.*

or what people do around us, but we do have control of what we choose to focus on.

> *Life is 10 percent what happens to us*
> *and 90 percent how we respond to it.*
> ~ Charles Swindoll

Your Attitude Determines Your Altitude

While writing this book, I found it interesting how many quotes there are to be found on this topic of attitude. It's been said that attitude is everything, and judging by the words of Charles Swindoll, he most certainly would agree. He said, "I believe the single most significant decision I can make on a day-to-day basis is my choice of attitude. It is more important than my past, my education, my bankroll, my successes or failures, fame or pain, what other people think of me or say about me, my circumstances, or my position. Attitude keeps me going or cripples my progress. It alone fuels my fire or assaults my hope. When my attitudes are right, there is no barrier too high, no valley too deep, no dream too extreme, no challenge too great for me."[5]

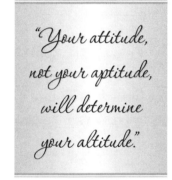

Zig Ziglar, who started with nothing and is now one of the most well-known motivational speakers of all time, often says, "Your attitude, not your aptitude, will determine your altitude." And I believe that entirely.

This certainly holds true where airplanes are concerned. My friend's husband is a pilot; he's also a minister. I once heard him say in a sermon that the *attitude* of a plane equals the rate of climb and the rate of ascent and descent. If the attitude is wrong, the plane will stall and can lose altitude…quickly!

Isn't the same true for us? If our attitude is wrong, it can cause us to stall and lose altitude. God wants us to fly. He wants us to soar like eagles. He wants to be the wind beneath our wings. But a normal day can quickly crash and burn when our attitude is sour. Conversely, a rotten day can be lifted when faced with a positive attitude.

Well then, if attitude is everything and can certainly affect everything, then I suppose it would be important to fully understand what an attitude is, where it originates from, and how to control and change it when necessary.

CHANGE YOUR MIND, CHANGE YOUR LIFE

An *attitude* is a state of mind that is formed by our thoughts and always results in a corresponding behavior.[6] So if you want to have

"We become what we think about."

a better attitude and you want to change your behavior, begin with thinking good thoughts—or more specifically, think God thoughts! The message in Proverbs 23:7 has been requoted many ways by many different people; Napoleon Hill said it this way: "We become what we think about."

Everything that comprises who and where we are right now began in the mind with a single thought. You know the great thing about that? If we're not completely pleased with who and where we are right now, we can begin to change that *with a single thought*.

Of course, this isn't a new idea. Thousands of years ago, Paul wrote:

> **Do not be conformed to this world, but be tranformed by the renewing of your mind.**
> ~ Romans 12:2 NKJV

Paul knew then what we, too, should grasp right now: In order for us to be transformed from the inside out, we must literally replace old thoughts with new ones—our old way of thinking with God's way of thinking. I like to call it "brainwashing." Yes, I know that's typically a negative term. However, I would suggest that a good brainwashing is exactly what you and I need—washing our minds in the water of the Word.

We have become so polluted by the ideals and mind-sets of this world, as we have been bombarded with them on television, movies, music, and billboards. We have slowly but surely been swayed into worldly beliefs, and because of that, we have skewed our focus. The lies of the world tell us that greed is the norm and perversion is acceptable. The world tells us that sex is for love, not just marriage and that the definition of a monogamous relationship means only that we are having sex with one partner at a time. The lies of the world have convinced us that we are not good enough, smart enough, or special enough to matter and that God's way is not the *only* way to live this life. These are the lies injected into this world by the enemy; and while we cannot change the mind-set of the entire world, we can certainly control *our own* mind-sets and attitudes. If we are ever going to move forward into the purposes of God, then we must reprogram our thinking to God's way of thinking. We must set our views apart from the world's view so we can begin to see the will of God more clearly.

The *New Living Translation* says it like this: "Don't copy the behavior and customs of this world, but let God transform you into a new person by changing the way you think. Then you will learn to know God's will for you, which is good and pleasing and perfect" (Rom. 12:2).

THE PROCESS BEGINS WITH YOU!

We've seen the enemy's process and its effects on the world around us (see chapter 2). Now it's time to learn about God's process of transformation and the effects it can have on the inside of us. First Chronicles 28:9 says, "For GOD examines every heart and sees through every motive. If you seek him, he'll make sure you find him" (MSG).

God wants you to find Him and to live out His perfect plan for your life. He wants to restore us from the inside out, but we have to be willing to cooperate with God in this process.

The process of changing our hearts, our minds, and our thoughts from the inside comes by intentionally getting in line with Him and seeing things as God sees them—from His perspective. Only when we see things as God sees them will we be willing to do as God says to do. This can only happen by renewing our minds and controlling our thought life. (In this chapter we will deal specifically with renewing the mind. In the next chapter we will deal heavily with controlling the thought life.)

Once we come to fully realize that we are God's and that He has forgiven us, called us, healed us, and delivered us from our former lives, then we will want to dedicate and devote our lives to doing as He desires for us. That begins with thinking as He would want us to think.

Charting a New Course

So just *how* do we renew our minds and change our mind-sets?

The answer? Only by the Word of God!

Second Timothy 3:16 states, "Every part of Scripture is God-breathed and useful one way or another—showing us truth, exposing our rebellion, correcting our mistakes, training us to live God's way." (MSG) The *Amplified Version* teaches that the word *God-breathed* actually means "given by His inspiration."

The Word of God has the ability to change our hearts, our minds, and our attitudes if we will let it. It's that powerful!

Setting—or Resetting Your Mind

I minister to people of all ages who repent of their sins, get free from their hurts and pains, but never determine to replace old mind-sets with new godly ones. The result? A floundering believer who, sooner rather than later, falls back into her old way of living. We must understand that simply owning a Bible isn't going to get the job done; we have to read it in order for it to do its work in us.

So let me tell you right now—if you intend to get free and *stay* free, then you *must* be willing to renew your mind by replacing the old lies with God's Truth. Think of it like reprogramming a computer. Once you delete the old, faulty information and input the new, correct information, you will have the correct information to draw from in the future. Reading and studying the Word of God is how you restore and reprogram your mind and its way of thinking—there really is no other way.

And let me also clarify: Renewing our minds is our responsibility, nobody else's. It doesn't happen by sitting underneath good preaching in church, nor does it happen automatically because we're saved. We must dig into God's Word for ourselves. God will lead us and guide us in His Truth, but we are the ones who must actively input the new that will replace the old. When we do, we will begin to change from the inside out.

The Word will work if you'll work it!

I promise you this: The Word will work if you'll work it! Use it! It will change your life!

IT'S TIME TO WORK IT!

Trying within our own strength to change our outward behavior is futile without first going to the root of the behavior. We're going to start at the source—changing your thought patterns and negative belief systems. You have your thoughts about God, yourself, and others on those cards. Now, let's do what's necessary to replace those ungodly thoughts with godly ones! Shall we? Take out those 3 x 5 cards again. It's time to renew our minds!

> *I want to know all God's thoughts; all the rest*
> *are just details.*
>
> ~ Albert Einstein

Let's start with the example we used in the beginning of this chapter: "I feel like God abandoned me at the time I needed Him the most! He wasn't there for me!" If those words were on the front of your card, then on the back of your card, we must find the Truth in God's Word to combat that lie. On the back of this particular

140

card, we could write the Scripture in Hebrews 13:5, making it personal to you.

front

I feel like God abandoned me at the time I needed Him the most! He wasn't there for me!

back

Hebrews 13:5 says God will never desert me nor forsake me! I know that He loves me and He has a good plan for my life. He is with me always!

Our other example might look like this:

front

No one—not even God—will ever be able to forgive me for what I have done. My life is ruined!

back

According to 1 John 1:9, when I confess my sins to God, He promises that He has forgiven me and cleanses me completely! And Jeremiah 29:11 says that God has a plan for my life, a plan for good and not disaster, to give me a future and a hope!

You will likely find multiple Scripture verses that apply to your mind-set. Choose the one(s) that speaks to you the most. And be sure to cite the Scripture location on your card so that you know where to find it in the Bible. This will help you with memorization, and it will help you to know where to find it so you can use it to minister to someone else in the future! After you write your interpretation of the Scripture, be sure to always write a declaration or revelation about that verse, such as: *God is not finished with me yet. He never gives up on me. He is patient and kind!*

Now do this with all of your cards—this will begin to help you replace old mind-sets that were founded on the enemy's lie with new mind-sets that are founded on God's Truth.

A really great place to spend some time is in replacing your negative thoughts of yourself with what *God* says about you. (See below for a list of Scriptures about you from God's Word.)

A new creation (2 Corinthians 5:17)
Complete through the union of Christ (Colossians 2:10)
Chosen (Deuteronomy 7:6 & 1 Thessalonians 1:4)
Beautiful and flawless (Song of Solomon 4:7)
An heir and joint heir with Christ (Romans 8:17)
A child of God (John 1:12)
Righteous and holy (Ephesians 4:24)
Accepted (Ephesians 1:6 NKJV)
Redeemed and forgiven of all sins (Colossians 1:13–14)
Loved completely and unconditionally (Romans 8:39)
Promised a wonderful future (Jeremiah 29:11)
Known and approved of by God (Jeremiah 1:5)
God's workmanship, created for good works (Ephesians 2:10)
Crowned with glory and honor (Psalm 8:3–5)

Loved with an everlasting love (Jeremiah 31:3)
The apple of God's eye (Psalm 17:8)
Fearfully and wonderfully made (Psalm 139:14)
These are God's Truths—the only truths that matter, the only truths we should allow to permeate our minds, and most definitely the only truths that should shape our attitudes.

For any other subject, if you don't know an applicable verse off the top of your head, go to the back of your Bible. There is almost always a concordance or index of specific topics, needs, or situations that you may be facing right now. Websites such as Bible.com or crosswalk.com are also great online resources where you can key in a word and it will pull up every place in the Bible where that subject is talked about. Begin getting into the Truth of God's Word this way, by looking up what God has to say on the subject. (This is called a topical or a word study.) You could use any number of methods, but this activity is just one way to begin to renew your mind and replace the lies with God's Truth.

Keep those cards handy and meditate on them daily and nightly (see Josh. 1:8) until they get engrained into your thoughts and mind! John Baker, in his book *Life's Healing Choices*, states that each time we think on a thought, whether positive or negative, it sends an electrical impulse across our brain that, with time and repetition, creates actual paths in our brain itself.[7] Repetitive negative, fear-based thoughts create literal ruts or pathways in the brain, but the good news is that thinking positive, faith-based thoughts can build new pathways and brain patterns in a very short period of time as well.

For the same reasons, Proverbs 4:20–22 tells us to pay attention and to listen carefully to God's words. He tells us not to lose sight of His words but to keep them front and center, allowing them to penetrate deep into our hearts. We are instructed to spend time with them, to consent to them by coming into agreement with His words, and to do as they say. We are told that doing this will bring life to us and healing to our whole body. Now that's a good enough reason for me!

Get into the Word of God for yourself, start reading about the character of God, and get to know His perspective on you, your life, and your future! Here are some tips on just how to get into the Word of God so that it can change you from the inside out:

1. **Change your perspective on God's Word.**

   We are not instructed to read the Bible because we are obligated. God isn't angry with us if we don't, and He isn't up there recording the time we spend in it. We read the Bible because it is God's Word to us, His guidance for us in this life (see 2 Tim. 3:16). It is spirit and life to us (see John 6:63); it is living and full of power (see Heb. 4:12). Second Corinthians 3:18 promises us that if we continue in it, we will be transformed by it. And because the Spirit of the Lord is in it, we become free by knowing it for ourselves (see John 8:31–32; 2 Cor. 3:17–18). We read it and study it to hear from God Himself about His perfect will and His undying love for us. We input its contents so that the Holy Spirit can remind us of the Truth when we need it—understanding fully that He can only remind us of what we already know. We hide the Word in our hearts so we will become aware of sin and choose not to go that direction (see Ps. 119:11) *and* because out of the abundance of the heart, the mouth speaks (see Matt. 12:34)—we're simply filling it up with God's Word!

2. **Get a Bible you can read and understand.**

   Everyone is different; therefore we prefer different versions of the Bible. My husband loves the King James Version with loads of commentaries on each page. He loves details and history, so he prefers in-depth teaching versions. I, on the other hand, am not detail oriented but I love versions that relate Scripture to my everyday life. Joyce Meyer has a great *Everyday Life Bible*. But when I get too bogged down by the *Amplified Version* (as that one is), I prefer the *New International Version*, the *Message*, or the *New American Standard Bible*.

When I first started reading the Bible, I began reading a real children's Bible in regular English. I knew nothing of the Bible, so I just really wanted to understand it and get familiar with the stories that I had never heard. A children's Bible was perfect for me. (I once heard Joyce Meyer say the same.) A great Bible for teens and young adults is one that reads like a magazine (called a Biblezine) but has full-Bible text in a teen-friendly translation. Whatever version you choose, choose one that you will understand and read because it appeals to you and your personality. The more you enjoy it, the more you will want to read it, and the more you will see results, so you'll keep reading!

3. **Check your heart before sitting down with the Word.**
   Pray before reading or studying His Word. As R. T. Kendall often instructs, we should be on good terms with its author! Go into it with right motives and a clean heart. And be sure you are going to the Word expecting to get something out of it!

4. **Take your time!**
   Don't get in a hurry. You're not punching a time clock here; you're learning and growing—and growth takes time! As I always say—it's about progress, not perfection. Set a specific time and place to meet with God, preferably daily. He's more interested in quality time than quantity of time, so

when you do spend time with Him, make it meaningful and focused.

5. **Know the difference between studying and reading—then do both!**

Some days, you might sit down to simply read for encouragement or for strength. Other days, you might sit down to study the Word more deeply. For instance, if you're struggling with impatience, then sit down and do a "word study" on patience from the Bible. Locate in the back of your Bible every place that it speaks about "patience" or "impatience." Then, go verse by verse, looking each Scripture up, writing it out, and meditating and reflecting on each one. Study it until you work the impatience out of you and the patience into you! You can do this with any topic—anger, greed, discouragement, jealousy, fear, guilt, shame, divorce, sorrow, adultery, loneliness, hope, healing—you name it, it's there! Word studies are exactly what I did to dig out from my own issues and gain a new perspective on my life. Try it. When you're studying, you may find it helpful to utilize other resources such as a *Strong's Concordance*, a *Thompson's Chain Reference Bible*, or a Bible dictionary. One great tool that makes topical studies easy is Steven K. Scott's book entitled *The Greatest Words Ever Spoken*, which breaks down by categories every word Jesus ever spoke about any given subject.

Second Timothy 2:15 tells us that we are to study the Word of God to make us approved and tried in our faith, founded in Truth. So do it! You'll come to really enjoy it!

Please believe me when I say that reading, praying, and studying the Word of God is the *only* way for us to change our attitudes, our behaviors, and our beliefs—about Him, about ourselves, and about others. I know. I've been there. I've tried every other way there is to try. I've experienced years of unnecessary suffering only to find that *there is only one way* to true healing and transformation. Don't skip it; don't even *skimp* on it. It *is* the way to complete healing.

Living in the Truth

John 8:32 tells us, "You will know the truth, and the truth will set you free." The word *know* in that verse is translated from the Hebrew word *ginosko*, which means to have knowledge of, perceive, or understand.[8] To perceive or understand, you must become intimate with it; you must become one with it! You see, it's not just the Truth that will make you free; the Truth has been there all along. It's what you *know* about the Truth that sets you free!

Psalm 139:14 says, "I praise you because I am fearfully and wonderfully made; your works are wonderful," and it ends with "I know that full well." In this case, the word *know* is translated from the Hebrew word *yada*, which means to perceive, to know by experience, to recognize, admit, acknowledge, and confess.[9] You must become intentional and repetitious with your new Truth. You must experience it. You must recognize it, admit it, acknowledge it, and *confess it.*

Look into your mirror and speak those Truths out loud to yourself every day and throughout the day. Do as King David and hide God's Word in your heart (see Ps. 119:11), meditate on it, think about it (see Ps. 119:15, 48, 78), declare it, and proclaim the Truths of God (see Ps. 63:6; 64:9; 73:28). Do so while you are brushing your teeth, on the way to work, as you walk or exercise. Write the Scriptures that speak to you personally on index cards (in addition to those you have already done) and place them around your house as reminders.

The more Truth you place inside of you, the stronger you will walk in the Truth, repelling the notions of the enemy. The Bible tells us that faith comes by hearing (see Rom. 10:17), and who better to hear it from than God Himself, from His Word, and then by your own mouth speaking it out loud as a declaration of Truth—until you learn to fully trust and believe in it!

That's what I was doing (unknowingly, at the time) that day in the bathroom at Disney. I was speaking life into myself, out loud. And even though I didn't even know *why* I was doing it, the effect was the same. The Bible tells us in Proverbs 18:21, "Death and life are in the power of the tongue" (NKJV). So start to proclaim life, speaking truth over yourself until it rises up inside of you and becomes the Truth that you base your life on, the Truth that you stand with and focus on daily, the Truth that *becomes* you!

ACKNOWLEDGE IT

1. Do you recognize that your negative behavior has been rooted in your negative beliefs and that your thoughts started it all? Can you list some of those behaviors you want to change? How can you change them?

2. Do you see the need to renew your mind by replacing old mind-sets with new ones—godly ones? What changes do you hope to see as a result?

3. What are your thoughts on getting into the Word for yourself? Does it intimidate you? Excite you? What are some of the feelings or thoughts that come to your mind when you think of reading and studying the Word? If your feelings are negative about reading and studying the Word, then perhaps your

feelings are based on a lie from the enemy! Examine them. Perhaps God can give you a new perspective on it as well!

Bring It to God

Lord, You know my attitudes and my beliefs have been terribly off! I have come to believe things that are not based upon Your Truth but upon the influences of the world and the lies of the enemy. I need You, Lord, to help me to change that. I will do my part by getting into Your Word for myself. Please help me to be diligent in it and enjoy it! I want to know You and to know Your Truth intimately. I need a new attitude, new mind-sets, and a new perspective. Help me daily to choose to stand with You and Your Truth. Amen.

Confess It

I will form a new attitude based on the Truths of God.

I see it now. My attitude has been way off! But that is changing with my new perspective and my new focus.

Admittedly, I've turned a deaf ear to God's Truths, allowing the enemy and the world to shape my beliefs about God, about myself, and about others. And as a result, I have developed an unhealthy attitude that has resulted in unhealthy behavior.

But now I know. I hear Him. And right now, I have begun to fill my heart with His Truths.

I will remind myself daily of the new Truth I have found in Him. I will allow those thoughts to permeate my entire being, to form a new attitude in my heart. I know that only then will my attitude toward God, myself, and others be one that glorifies God and allows me to step into the purpose He has for me.

God loves me, I am accepted, and I have the power and the strength to choose how I respond to others. God is changing me from the inside out—by His Word!

I have a new attitude.

Who ever asked you to feel?

You were chosen to be a princess!

Now go...

Wash your face...

Get a new attitude...

Put on your clothes...

And go be Cinderella!

CHAPTER 7

"Put on Your Clothes"

PRINCESS PRINCIPLE #6:
STEP INTO THE SHOES MADE ONLY FOR YOU.

Put on the new self, created after the likeness of God
in true righteousness and holiness.
~ EPHESIANS 4:24 ESV

"I can do this. I'm a princess."

I reminded myself of that all the way out of the bathroom, down the hall where I picked up my costume, and into the greenroom to dress for my Cinderella set.

I did as Tommy said: I got dressed, all the while repeating to myself, "I can do this...I *have* to do this...I'm a princess..."

I must have repeated it a hundred times. I said it to myself, as my wig was being placed onto my throbbing head and styled to perfection. I repeated it as my makeup was meticulously applied. And I was still repeating it when I was transformed by stepping into the clothes of a princess.

Most little girls I know love dressing up and becoming Cinderella (or in my daughter Jordan's case, Hannah Montana). And as adults, don't we still play dress up? We may spend a little extra time on our appearance, add a little glisten to our skin, apply a darker lipstick, or even slip into a new outfit to go out for the evening with our husbands or out on the town with a friend. We paint our nails, get a pedicure, and instantly we feel better about ourselves. We walk a bit more confidently, speak a bit more purposefully, and eat a little more refined than usual—maybe even sticking out our pinky finger while drinking our beverage during dinner.

There's definitely something about putting on nice clothes or a new outfit that helps us to gain a fresh, new perspective about ourselves. And I think we can all attest to the fact that dressing "frumpy" (as my mom calls it) and not taking the best care of ourselves definitely has the opposite effect. We walk much differently in old, stinky house slippers than we do in patent-leather heels.

Consider the number of "makeover" reality shows that you've seen on TV. People love that stuff! Women (and men) are fascinated by the transformation of a woman who doesn't take care of herself into a beautiful, poised woman who walks confidently out from behind a curtain into a crowd of friends who are shedding tears of joy and amazement! The beauty was there all along, but it took a new haircut, a facial, and a few new outfits to bring it out.

A new look has literally transformed her from the outside in. And as we watch, we wonder if we, too, fix the outside, will the inside fall in line with what the outside is portraying?

I believe actors would say that, yes, portraying a character very much depends upon dressing the part. Jim Carey endured three hours in makeup every day just to play the role of the Grinch. Actors sometimes endure ten or twelve *hours* in makeup getting prepared to *become* the character that they are portraying in a movie. (Some mornings, I'm lucky if I get to spend ten or twelve *minutes!*)

I know that for me, each time I stepped into my costume or into my Cinderella shoes, I seemed to *become* my character. The clothes I put on for each role gave me a new mind-set as I stepped into them—and never more so than that day when Tommy told me to go "put on" my Cinderella costume and get to work. In a sense, he was telling me to go "put on" my new mind-set and become what I was called there to be.

So, is there anything to this theory? Or is it just a meaningless, superficial practice that wastes our time and resources? Well, if you ask me, I say there *is* something real to it.

Now, I'm not talking about going out and spending money that we don't have in a compulsive attack of escapism spending. I'm simply speaking of *dressing* the part of who we are in the Lord. And perhaps the importance of "putting on" something on the outside is *not* just a theory—perhaps it's a biblical concept!

After doing a little "word study" during my study time one day, I discovered nearly fifty instances where someone was either instructed to *put on* something or did *put on* something specific in order to fill a role or to accomplish a particular deed for God.

Of those instances, I discovered that for each of the biblical subjects we've been discussing—Aaron, David, Esther, and Ruth—there was, in fact, the act of *putting on* their garments before going into their destinies as well. Remember, they all washed, anointed themselves to get a new attitude, and then *put on* their clothes. And with Aaron, God gave him specific instructions about what to wear, or what to *put on* as his priestly garments.

Why is that? Why would God be so specific as to include it in the Scripture we've studied about them? I wholeheartedly feel that it is part of the process of stepping into our purpose.

So why is *what* we "put on" so important to the process?

I believe our answer can be found in understanding what *put on* means in biblical terms. In Aaron's story, Leviticus 8 describes Aaron putting on his new priestly garments (see Lev. 8:7,12). If we dig a little more, we will find that *put on* has three distinct meanings that shed some light on the importance of what we *put on*.

The words *put on* can mean:

1. Array—to place in order
2. Armor—to arm against
3. Apparel—to cover, to wrap around, to become one with, or *sink into*[1]

In this chapter, we're going to break down each of those meanings together and explore what God is requiring us to *put on* to fill our roles and to step into our shoes that were only made for us.

Let's start with the word *array* or "to place in order." As I began to study those words and reflect on the words of Tommy that day, I realized that when Tommy instructed me to put on my clothes after telling me to get a new attitude, he was essentially telling me to get my priorities in order and to step into my character.

And that is precisely what God is calling us to do now. We must get things in order for the journey ahead and step into our new character.

OLD THOUGHTS, NEW YOU!

Second Corinthians 5:17 says, "Therefore if any man be in Christ, he is a new creature: old things are passed away; behold, all things are become new" (KJV).

I can remember the first time I came across this Scripture in my reading as I was earnestly trying to renew my mind and convince myself of my newfound worth and value in Christ. When I first read this, I almost laughed out loud! *Boy*, I thought, *I might be a new creature in Christ, but I sure do still feel like the old creature is within me alive and kicking!*

I knew in my mind I was saved, but my thoughts and my feelings were not exactly lining up with my new way of how I was supposed to be thinking and acting. Despite my desire to truly change, I was still wrestling with impure thoughts, jealousies, anger, and much of the time, I was still longing to go back into my old behaviors and lifestyle. All of those old desires hadn't instantly gone away, and the more I tried to focus on doing what I know God would want me to do, the more I thought about just going back and selling out! Then, the more I dwelled on them and the more I contemplated that maybe God was mad at me for thinking about them, the more I felt confused and emotionally exhausted from the struggle.

Despite my desire to truly change, I was still wrestling with impure thoughts and old behaviors.

Then, by the love and the grace of God, I was reading one day in the book of Romans, and I discovered another person in God's Word who sounded as crazy as I felt! His name is Paul, and as I later came to understand, he was a strong believer and dedicated follower of Christ who wrote two-thirds of the New Testament. His original name, though, was Saul, and prior to becoming a believer, was a murderer and a man full of pride and anger against followers of Christ! The specific part that really spoke to me is found in Romans 7:14–24. He wrote this portion when he was already following and serving God.

> *"I know that all God's commands are spiritual, but I'm not. Isn't this also your experience?"*
>
> *Yes. I'm full of myself—after all, I've spent a long time in sin's prison. What I don't understand about myself is that I decide one way, but then I act another, doing things I absolutely despise. So if I can't be trusted to figure out what is best for myself and then do it, it becomes obvious that God's command is necessary. ...For if I know the law but still can't keep it, and if the power of sin within me keeps sabotaging my best intentions, I obviously need help! I realize that I don't have what it takes. I can will it, but I can't do it. I decide to do good, but I don't really do it; I decide not to do bad, but then I do it anyway. My decisions, such as they are, don't result in actions. Something has gone wrong deep within me and gets the better of me every time.*
>
> *It happens so regularly that it's predictable. The moment I decide to do good, sin is there to trip me up. I truly delight in God's commands, but it's pretty obvious that not all of me joins in that delight. Parts of me covertly rebel, and just when I least expect it, they take charge.*
>
> *I've tried everything and nothing helps. I'm at the end of my rope. Is there no one who can do anything for me?*
> (MSG)

Wow! Did I instantly feel better about my own insanity! Paul was like me and perhaps like you too. He loved God, desired to follow Him with his whole heart, but still struggled within himself to think right thoughts and do right things. He understood that we are spiritual beings, saved by grace, but living in fleshly bodies with souls that need restoring—and minds that need constant renewing! He was constantly trying to keep his thoughts in order with his new character.

I rejoiced that night that the Holy Spirit had Paul to write those verses into the Bible so that you and I could see that there is nothing *wrong* with us or messed up about us when we experience these thoughts. We should breathe a little easier after reading this but also realize that this does not necessarily give us permission to remain this way. We should recognize the problem so we can do what is necessary to fix our thinking and control the flesh that wants to control us and keep us confused in our journey with the Lord.

> *We are spiritual beings, living in fleshly bodies with minds that need constant renewing!*

In the end, Paul finally came to the conclusion that you and I must come to as well. It's the answer to the question of whether or not there is anyone who can help us. In verse 25 he finally concludes, "The answer, thank God, is that Jesus Christ can and does" (MSG). He is our only hope. He's the only One who can change us.

IF ONLY SOMEONE HAD TOLD ME...

I'm about to let you in on something I wish someone had taken the time to teach me earlier on in my relationship with the Lord. Here goes: Just because we're saved and we are standing with Christ certainly does not mean that we are now off-limits to the enemy's assault against our minds. Quite the contrary, I'm afraid! It is now, during the process of renewing our minds and discovering the real Truth, that he will aggressively try to interfere with our progress!

Ephesians 6:12 tells us that we are engaged in a battle—a battle that is not "against flesh-and-blood enemies, but against evil rulers and authorities of the unseen world, against mighty powers in this dark world, and against evil spirits in the heavenly places" (NLT). Satan is our enemy, and he is battling for our souls. As we discussed in chapter 2, the enemy is out to reap our eternity apart from God. He hates us because we are followers of Christ, but do not worry. God loves us unconditionally, and we have nothing to fear with God on our side. The Bible tells us that God's Spirit is in us and He is greater than the enemy who is in the world (see 1 John 4:4)!

> *God loves us unconditionally, and we have nothing to fear with God on our side.*

I say that not to alarm you but because it's important that we recognize that following Christ as a believer is not a game to be played haphazardly. Because we belong to God, our spirit is reborn, but we are still in the process of renewing our minds with the Word of God and taking control of our fleshly desires. This is an ongoing process—a journey—that takes time, effort, attention, and strength from the Lord.

Our mind is the battleground on which the enemy wages war against us, our faith, and our newfound freedoms, so we must learn how to fight to keep our minds free of all those ungodly thoughts that we've discussed. We must daily wage war against the thoughts that infiltrate our minds and weaken our faith. We must continue to renew our minds daily with His Word to stay focused on the things of God, keeping a proper perspective so we are not led astray so easily.

Now the Good News

Okay, so by now you're thinking, *More work to do? What happened to just believing in God?*

Well, I cannot tell a lie: This next step, putting your thoughts in order—actively controlling your thought life—is the biggest job of all! And it can feel like a full-time job at first. (After all, it is said that we think up to sixty thousand thoughts a day!) But the good news is, once we learn how to do it and we begin implementing these practical steps, they will enable us to walk with freedom and clarity every day so that we can live and enjoy the life that God has for us. So it is a job that is well worth the time and the effort! And it's a job that gets easier and easier with every day you put it into practice. I promise!

Sure, it may sound easier to simply justify that we are saved now and just get by as so many do—religiously sitting on a church pew every Sunday, not knowing squat about the Bible or making any concerted effort to change. But let me ask you this: Which would you rather do? Would you rather continue in your old irrational way of thinking and behaving, riding the roller coaster of emotions daily, struggling with thoughts and being tormented by feelings of guilt, inadequacy, and inferiority while lashing out at the ones you love and damaging the relationships that matter most to you? Or would you rather put in the time and the effort to once and for all learn how to completely replace the faulty mind-sets that have led to destructive behaviors and painful consequences, control the thoughts that normally make you unable to cope with everyday life, and work diligently and consistently right now on renewing your mind so you can get free and stay free of all the pains, shame, and emptiness that you have had to deal with?

I thought so! So let's get started with putting our thought lives in order, or as some say, getting the mind of Christ (see 1 Cor. 2:16).

STRATEGIES FOR PUTTING YOUR THOUGHTS IN ORDER

1. **Continue to renew your mind daily.**

    Aside from the Bible itself, there are loads of tremendous resources available that can help you to renew your mind. (See the back of this book for a listing of some that have helped me over the years). The more you know God's Truth, the more the lie of the enemy will be that much more easily recognized and therefore more easily and quickly dealt with as well. God's Word is working on the inside of you even when you don't see it.

2. **Cast down all lies immediately!**

    When a thought comes into your mind that you recognize as a lie, do as Second Corinthians 10:3–5 says and cast it down and out immediately. (This practice of stopping my thoughts and casting them down changed my life—truly!) Because our war is spiritual, we cannot fight like we would a physical, natural battle; we must fight with God's Word against the enemy just as Jesus did in the wilderness (see Matt. 4). When a thought comes in that is a lie, stop it and override it with the Truth. Verse 5 says that we are to "destroy arguments and every lofty opinion raised against the knowledge of

> *When a thought comes in that is a lie, stop it and override it with the Truth.*

God, and take every thought captive to obey Christ" (ESV). Do this: Imagine in your mind a thought coming in that is contrary to God's Word. The moment you recognize it, stop it, reach up, pull it down, and give it over to the Lord, saying, *Nope, this one isn't from You, God. I'm not thinking on it!* This is an exercise I've done for years. Reach up, pull it down, and hand it over to God immediately. It's not to be thought about, considered, or evaluated for one second. If it's a lie, don't even waste your time with it!

3. **Stay on offense, not defense!**

   This is one of the biggest tricks of the enemy—to keep you fighting with him all day so you won't be able to focus on God! As long as you're playing defense, you won't have the strength or the focus to enjoy life and see what God has in store for you each day. So refocus! Philippians 4:8 tells us to "Fix your thoughts on what is true, and honorable, and right, and pure, and lovely, and admirable. Think about things that are excellent and worthy of praise" (NLT).

> *Thinking is the talking of the soul with itself.*
>
> ~ Plato

4. **Think about what you're thinking about.**

   Remember: Where your mind goes, your body follows. So don't allow your mind to wander aimlessly without giving thought to what you're thinking about. Mark 14:38 says it this way: "Stay alert, be in prayer, so you don't enter the danger zone without even knowing it. Don't be naive. Part of you is eager, ready for anything in God; but another part is as lazy as an old dog sleeping by the fire" (MSG). Other versions say that the spirit is willing but the flesh is weak—stay on guard of your thoughts! If you find yourself thinking on something that is leading you astray and you stumble, then stop and ask yourself the question: *What led to that behavior? What triggered that thought?* Perhaps something in your environment triggered that thought and led you astray—which leads me to my next point…

5. **Simplify your life: Clear your pathway!**

   Several years ago, I was struggling over the same thoughts that repetitively caused me grief and caused me to stumble. I was a lot like Ashley from chapter 2—the girl who reminisced about her past relationships when she got weak and took out her "box of memories." Despite my true love for my husband and desire to not look back to my old life, the enemy kept my mind going back to former boyfriends and past relationships. Many of them would even call my mom's house asking for me, not knowing I'd been married (that's what happens when you run off and get married in eight short weeks!) I was constantly struggling to stay focused on my marriage and my husband, but I was constantly feeling guilty for my thoughts. It was more than a nuisance—it was torture! Finally, God revealed to me that there were certain triggers around my house that kept me tied to my past: old photos, clothes that boyfriends had bought me, and the like. God spoke to me one day through an illustration in my mind. He showed me that I was trying to walk along this straight path, but every now and again I would trip over this huge boulder in my way. He said to me, *If you'll move the boulder out of your pathway, you'll stop tripping over it!* That was all I needed. I immediately threw away everything that triggered those thoughts.

   Remember that the soul is comprised of our will, imagination, intellect, emotions, and memory. For me, the enemy was using those pictures and such to activate old memories that were tied to emotions that led me to struggle. It wasn't that I didn't love my husband; it was that my emotions were being played by the enemy.

So be aware of his tactics. If you constantly trip over something, clear the pathway! If pornography is a struggle, then cancel your subscription or get a lock on your computer. If you struggle with gossiping about others, don't answer the phone when fellow gossipers call! If you struggle with your self-esteem, then stop looking at magazines and comparing yourself to airbrushed photos of models who haven't eaten in a week!

What you feed will grow; what you starve will die.

You get my point. If your flesh is weak, don't make any provisions for it (see Rom. 13:14). Clear out the external triggers and influences from your life. Live in a bubble if you must until you get stronger! What you feed will grow; what you starve will die. Starve the habit! Clean out your environment and cut yourself a break!

6. **Take it one day at a time with Jesus!**

Be realistic with your growth! This is a daily process! Just as you wouldn't throw out a newborn baby for his inability to walk, don't be quick to throw yourself under a bus for not being perfect! Changing our old habits and overhauling our thought lives takes time and patience. Don't get discouraged or in a hurry. Take it one day at a time, one thought at a time.

And remember you can do all things with Jesus (see Phil. 4:13). God does not expect perfection out of you;

that's why He provided a perfect Savior, Jesus, for us. Galatians 2:16 says, "Convinced that no human being can please God by self-improvement, we believed in Jesus as the Messiah so that we might be set right before God by trusting in the Messiah, not by trying to be good" (MSG). Changing your thoughts and behaviors is not something we are working on to be "good" or to get God to love us, but rather it is *because* of His love for us and our love for Him that we want to be our best for Him. He couldn't love us any more than He already does. Realize that perfection is not going to be achieved but progress is—but only if we look to Him.

THE *IF, THEN* PRINCIPLE

Under God's plan, thoughts are not the only things that have to be brought into order. Our actions need to be in order as well. We are also required to take steps toward becoming the person God is calling us to be so that the situations in our lives can then begin coming into alignment, or order, with what God wants our lives to be.

I have ministered to many frustrated women who desperately want God to work on their failing marriages, stubborn husbands, and seemingly hopeless relationships. They are praying that God will "fix" their husbands. All the while they are firmly standing their ground, digging in their heels and saying, "When he starts treating me better, *then* I will start treating him with the respect he wants." They are waiting for their husbands to change *first* before they start doing and becoming the wife God is calling them to be.

In many areas of life, we stubbornly wait for everything that is out of order in our lives to miraculously come into proper order and alignment *before* we will begin doing our part to make the situation better. We dig our heels and protest that we are not being treated as we believe we should be or that life is not going in our favor. We determine in our hearts that we will not budge until things start to change first! In these types of standoffs, as you probably know, there is seldom a winner.

Perhaps we should consider a different approach—an approach more likely to produce positive results and more likely to gain God's assistance. Believe me, I know what it is to feel as though I'm doing all the giving while the other party is doing all the taking. It isn't easy to continue trying while the other person doesn't seem to try at all. But remember, if God is going to be able to work on our behalf, we have to be in line with His Word and doing what He commands and expects of us—*first*.

"But that's not fair," we cry.

Maybe not...but in doing so, we are telling God that we trust His ways, we are in line with His Word, and we are placing our situation in His able hands to do what only He can do—change the heart of a person.

Isaiah 55:8–9 says, "'My thoughts are nothing like your thoughts,' says the Lord. 'And my ways are far beyond anything you could imagine. For just as the heavens are higher than the earth, so my ways are higher than your ways and my thoughts higher than your thoughts'" (NLT).

A WAKE-UP CALL FROM MY WALMART GUY

Several years ago, I had just given birth to my first child, a beautiful (and huge) baby boy whom we named Bradley "Cole." As joyous as we were over his birth, it was absolutely devastating to me that I'd gained over sixty pounds (more than double the amount of recommended weight gain) during my pregnancy. I'd had the baby, but the weight was still there!

Honestly, the weight itself wasn't the biggest problem. I knew that I was heavy, but even more than that, I knew how I'd gotten there. I was again bound to an eating disorder that had nearly taken my life just a few years prior. I was alone and in pain. As the saying goes: Eating disorders aren't as much about how much food you consume, but rather how much food consumes you.

Unmistakably—I was completely consumed. Food was the first thing I thought about when I woke up in the morning, and the last thing I thought about when I went to bed, not to mention all the hours in between. If I wasn't thinking about eating, I was thinking about not eating. The more miserable and depressed I became, the more I buried my pain under more food. Soon everything in my life was out of order—which incidentally is exactly what the word *disorder* means. Everything began falling apart!

Knowing that I couldn't continue to live like this, I decided to get serious with God in prayer. Night after night, I would sit and rock my newborn baby, praying that God would deliver me. When he was asleep, I would sit alone in my chair and just cry. When no one was around, I would lie facedown on the floor and plead for God to help me. I had been asking God to deliver me and change me, day after day, week after week, but there was no answer. It was like God just wasn't hearing me!

One afternoon, in all of my misery, I decided to leave the baby with my mom and escape to do some retail therapy—something else I knew better than to do! But it was there in Walmart that something defining happened that would forever change my outlook on prayer.

Anthony and I were in the check-out line just waiting for our groceries to be rung up when a friend of my husband's came walking up to us in line. I can't really tell you his name. I just called him "the Walmart guy" because that's the only place we would ever see him. He didn't work there; we just happened to run into him almost every time we were there shopping.

Anyway, he walked up to Anthony, put his hand on his shoulder, and said, "Good to see ya, man!" Then looking over at me, pointing at my (still) enormous belly, he said words I'll never forget. "Hey, not much longer, huh?"

To his credit, it only took him a moment to realize that he had stuck his foot so far down his throat that neither he nor I could breathe. Everything seemed to stand still. It was all the nosey cashier could do not to look up and stare. The Walmart guy's eyes were as big as saucers at both his blunder and, I'm sure, the look on my face. My knuckles were turning white and my eyes welled up with tears. I had a vision of myself literally leaping over the cart between us and pummeling the man half to death.

My complete concentration was now focused on writing that check and getting out of there before I broke. I knew that, given my already unstable frame of mind and roller-coaster emotions, I needed to just get to the car. The sooner the better. I tried desperately not to look at anyone—especially Walmart guy. I'm not sure what I wanted to do worse: scream, hurt him, or squall like a baby. Actually, I wanted to do all three!

But then—somewhere between the double exit doors of Walmart and my parked SUV—God spoke to me in an undeniable way. Almost instantly, I was reminded of every tear I'd shed about my eating disorder and every prayer I'd prayed concerning my weight gain. I could literally see myself lying facedown on my floor in tears, crying out for God to help me! Then, as we began unloading our groceries, He brought my attention to all of the junk I'd just purchased at Walmart—cookies, ice cream, desserts . . .

And at that moment an all-too-familiar Scripture went scrolling through my mind—one I'd preached dozens of times before—the one found in Second Chronicles 7:14: "If my people, who are called by my name, will humble themselves and pray and seek my face and turn from their wicked ways, then will I hear from heaven and will forgive their sin and will heal their land."

I knew exactly what He was telling me!

Later that night, I got alone with God, and He was kind enough to illuminate two very important words to me in this Scripture: *if* and *then*. As He pointed out, that passage didn't say that God would hear from heaven, forgive their sins, and heal their land, and all they would have to do is sit there and look pretty while praying about it. No, it said *if* the people of God would do four things—1) humble themselves, 2) pray, 3) seek His face, and 4) turn from their wicked ways—*then* God would do three things that they were asking: 1) hear, 2) forgive, and 3) heal their land.

In other words, *if* I wanted to be delivered, and *if* I wanted to lose weight, *then* I would have to eat differently. *If* I were going to change, *then* I would have to get off of my complaining, excuse-making backside and *do* something about it. God wanted to help me, but He was not going to come down, buy my groceries for me, and spoon-feed me what I needed to eat. That was my job. Praying for weight loss was pointless if my prayer was followed by a pint of Ben & Jerry's ice cream!

OUR ACTIONS HAVE TO BE CONSISTENT WITH OUR PRAYERS

You see, I was asking God to deliver me of my food addiction, then telling Him to keep away from my food! It's kind of like that porn addict asking God for deliverance, yet refusing to give up his favorite magazine or lock up his computer. Or a person diagnosed with lung cancer asking God for healing while continuing to smoke three packs of cigarettes a day. Or an unfaithful wife asking God to improve her marriage but not being willing to end her extramarital affair. God wants to help us, but we have to be willing to do our part. I've heard it said this way: If we'll do what we *can* do, then God will do what we *can't* do!

There are things that are required of us before we can expect God to intervene. This is not because God wants to exercise dictatorship over us; He simply wants us to turn to Him and trust Him. It is through our obedience to God's commands that we show Him that we love Him, that we trust Him, and that we are ready and willing for Him to come into our situation and do His part. And when we do that, then and only then can we fully expect that He will show up, being faithful to His Word, and work on our behalf.

We have to *put on, become,* or *place things in proper order* in our own lives by doing what we can do so that God can do what we can't.

James 1:22 tells us to "be doers of the word, and not hearers only" (NKJV). We are to obey God's Word, not just hear it, not just pray about it. Now, I know that prayer is powerful, and prayer can change everything, but I also know that we sometimes use prayer as a means to procrastinate. Sometimes, the things that we have the ability to change and the things we have the ability to make happen for ourselves just don't ever get done. Instead of us putting some "feet on our prayers" by finding our answer in His Word and doing what it tells us to do, we just sit around and pray about it. That is not God's way!

Everything we need is in His Word. Every answer to any question can be found in the Bible if we will just look. But we must not only look, we must obey it once we find it.

All throughout the Bible are promises and commands that are, as I call them, if-then statements. Not all of them start with the words *if* and *then*, but they all give us specific instruction on how, if we'll follow their direction, to get the situations in our lives fixed. These Scriptures tell us that there are things first required of us before we can expect God to intervene on our behalf. Let's look at some of them:

To receive the gift of salvation	Romans 10:9	*If* you believe and confess, *then* you will be saved.
To be forgiven	1 John 1:9	*If* you confess your sins, *then* He will forgive you and cleanse you completely.
For opportunities in your life	Matthew 7:7	*If* you ask, *then* you shall receive.
For marital help	Ephesians 5:22–25	*If* you become the spouse you're called to be, *then* God can work on the heart of your spouse.
For financial help	Malachi 3:8–10	*If* you follow His Word about finances, *then* He will pour out uncontainable blessings. (Notice also in this Scripture that *if* we will follow His instructions, *then* He promises to rebuke the devourer for our sakes as well.)
For winning friends	Proverbs 18:24	*If* we show ourselves friendly, *then* we will gain friends.
To mend foolish decisions	Proverbs 6:1–5	*If* you humble yourself in bad decisions, *then* you will be delivered from them.
To gain a closer walk with Jesus	James 4:8	*If* you will draw closer to Him, *then* He will drawer closer to you!

Many of the things we lose sleep over, many of the issues, problems, and wounds we cry over are self-inflicted. We make decisions that cause ourselves trouble and then think that with one prayer, God is required to come to our rescue and mend what we have broken, without any further effort on our part. We often expect God to fix in an instant what took us years to mess up. Then, we have the nerve to get upset when He doesn't do it, or doesn't do it *when* or *how* we want it done!

So don't wait for things to change on their own and don't declare a standoff. Begin to place in order—begin to *put on, array*—those things that have been out of order in your life and start becoming your best you! God has given us the Holy Spirit to teach us and guide us (see 1 Cor. 2:13). His supply is endless. But we must do our part as well. We are co-laborers with the Lord (see 1 Cor. 3:9). Sometimes…He's just waiting on us!

Arm Yourself, Princess!

Once we get into alignment with God's order of things, following His Word and doing our part by becoming who He expects us to become, we must then arm ourselves against the enemy and those who are out to deter us, knowingly or unknowingly, from God's plan, those who keep us from God's best. "To arm," the second definition of *put on*, means that we must go on the defensive to keep ourselves on the right track and preserve our freedoms.

Ephesians 6:13–18 tells us to arm ourselves with the whole armor of God:

> *Be prepared. You're up against far more than you can handle on your own. Take all the help you can get, every weapon God has issued, so that when it's all over but*

the shouting you'll still be on your feet. Truth, righteousness, peace, faith, and salvation are more than words. Learn how to apply them. You'll need them throughout your life. God's Word is an indispensable weapon. In the same way, prayer is essential in this ongoing warfare. Pray hard and long. Pray for your brothers and sisters. Keep your eyes open. Keep each other's spirits up so that no one falls behind or drops out (MSG).

Let's break down some tips to arm ourselves properly:

1. **Pray constantly!**
   Luke 21:34–36 says it this way: "But be on your guard.... Pray constantly that you will have the strength and wits to make it through everything that's coming and end up on your feet before the Son of Man" (MSG).

2. **Choose your friends wisely!**
   Examine your relationships and associations. People can either be your biggest help or your greatest hindrance.

3. **Stay in the Word.**
   It is the light that will illuminate your path (see Ps. 119:105).

4. **Flee—run from—temptation!**
   God promises not to allow anything to overtake you unless you just let it! He always provides a way of escape—it's called "choice"! When you call on Him, He will never let you down (see 1 Cor. 10:13).

5. **Arm yourself with resources.**
   There are thousands of well-written, well-versed, Bible-based resources out there—in addition to God's Word itself—to aid you in your quest for freedom from your issues and knowledge for your journey. There are ministries out there with great teachings on just about anything, books

on every topic you can think of, and CDs and DVDs for those who would rather watch and listen than read. Utilize resources. The old saying "Knowledge is power" is true! Get some!

6. **Get an accountability partner.**

Just as we said in previous chapters, find a strong friend who is headed in the same godly direction as you—who can smack some spiritual sense into you if you're headed off course! Don't do it alone. We need each other! Ecclesiastes 4:9–10 says, "Two people are better off than one, for they can help each other succeed. If one person falls, the other can reach out and help. But someone who falls alone is in real trouble" (NLT).

> ***Accountability is a willingness to***
> ***explain your actions.***
> ~ Chuck Swindoll

DON YOUR APPAREL

The third and final meaning of *put on* is one we are all familiar with—to *put on apparel*. "Putting on" apparel is to say that when we step into it, as it covers us, we become one with it or sink into it until it *becomes* us. We all know what it is to put on a costume or some piece of apparel that helps us transform ourselves into another character, don't we? Remember stepping into a costume as a child? There's nothing like it! Just ask Cole, my nine-year-old son. I suppose I had a lot to do with his obsession with costumes and becoming the latest, greatest superhero. When he was just three months old, I was tooling around Walmart when I came across the cutest Superman and Batman shorts sets, complete with full capes on the backs and superhero insignias on the front. I just had to buy them for him. I loved them so much that I bought him the outfits in every size from 3–6 months to 3T!

When Cole was old enough to become acquainted with the characters and the cartoons and movies behind the costumes, he *became* the characters—in full garb, every day! His fascination with it became so intense that he wanted to wear the outfit every single day of the week. I found myself washing the outfits every night before bed, just so they would be clean for him to wear the next day.

Finally, I got so tired of washing them every night that I went back to Walmart and bought four of each outfit—a total of eight costumes to wear throughout the week (four Superman and four Batman).

He wore them constantly. He went to the store in them, slept in them, played in them, and even went to church in them. I wasn't overly concerned with the obsession because he was fully aware that his name was Cole, not Superman, and that he was not actually the character himself. Well, at least not until he put his cape on!

Cinderella was another great story of transformation. She was an ordinary girl, who probably was not feeling too great about her circumstances. Her stepmother and stepsisters forced her to do all of the cooking and cleaning. Daily she dressed in rags, covered in soot and ashes. In spite of such lowly circumstances, she continued to believe that one day her prince would come—that she was destined for more than being a servant to her stepfamily. She kept a positive attitude and behaved as a princess long before she became one.

Ah, and then comes her fairy godmother. With a bouncy little tune and the wave of a magic wand—*poof!*—Cinderella was dressed head-to-toe in the attire of a princess. And of course, as the story goes, the dressed-up Cinderella goes to the ball and captures the heart of Prince Charming. She was the same girl all along—but suddenly, in the new gown and glass slippers, she steps into the role of princess.

FAKE IT 'TIL YOU MAKE IT!

Well, that's what the world calls it. God simply calls it walking by faith, being our best, doing what's right even when it feels wrong.

There's definitely something to be said for this concept of "dressing the part" or putting on who we *want* to become. It's all throughout the Bible.

The Bible actually tells us that we are to put on several things. Let's quickly run through them: We are to put on Christ, righteousness, the armor of God (as we learned earlier), love,

> *In spite of such lowly circumstances, she kept a positive attitude and behaved as a princess long before she became one.*

strength, and our "new self" (see Eph. 4:24). But it only stands to reason that before we can put anything on, we must first take something off, right?

Let's look at verse 22: "Put off your old self, which belongs to your former manner of life and is corrupt through deceitful desires" (ESV). We've been doing a lot of that already, so we're ahead of the game!

I love how plainly Colossians 3:8–10 says it in *The Message*:

> *And that means killing off everything connected with that way of death: sexual promiscuity, impurity, lust, doing whatever you feel like whenever you feel like it, and grabbing whatever attracts your fancy. That's a*

life shaped by things and feelings instead of by God. It's because of this kind of thing that God is about to explode in anger. It wasn't long ago that you were doing all that stuff and not knowing any better. But you know better now, so make sure it's all gone for good: bad temper, irritability, meanness, profanity, dirty talk. Don't lie to one another. You're done with that old life. It's like a filthy set of ill-fitting clothes you've stripped off and put in the fire. Now you're dressed in a new wardrobe.

In other words, get dressed! Put on your new character. It's time to walk the walk and talk the talk! James 4:8 says it this way: "Quit dabbling in sin. Purify your inner life. Quit playing the field. Hit bottom, and cry your eyes out. The fun and games are over. Get serious, really serious. Get down on your knees before the Master; it's the only way you'll get on your feet" (MSG). Become what He has called you to be.

> *Put on your new character. It's time to walk the walk and talk the talk!*

We are "to put on the new self, created after the likeness of God in true righteousness and holiness" (Eph.4:24 ESV). To *put on righteousness* means that we step into each day with a pure heart before God, knowing that we are in right standing not because of what we've done but because of what He's done—that is what it means to *put on Christ*. He sacrificed Himself for us so that we can be free from condemnation and fear of God's judgment. It means that we are to wake up each morning reminding ourselves that we are picked out specifically by God, chosen by Him to be His adopted children in Christ, loved unconditionally, and given a perfect heart—this is how we *put on strength* for the journey. But it also means that we recognize that we are never going to be able to achieve perfect behavior and perfect performance as long as we're in this world. God knew us when He chose us, and He knows us better than we know ourselves. He knows it's impossible within ourselves to walk perfectly in this life. That's why He provided us with the Holy Spirit—to lead us and guide us into a relationship with Him through Jesus Christ (see Gal. 5:16). If we are to be and become who God intends us to be, we should be reaching out to do good—that's what it means to *put on love*. We *put on love* by seeking out good to do for others. (see 1 Thess. 5:15) It means we become the hands, arms, and feet of Jesus by doing what He taught us when He was on the earth—to extend God's love and grace to all we come in contact with. That is what it means to *put on our new self*!

PUT ON YOUR PURPOSE!

Knowing some of these elements of "putting on," we must finally *put on* our special purpose; we must dress in who we are to become in Christ daily.

It is imperative that we step into the shoes that were only made for us. Just as Cinderella's fairy godmother formed those glass slippers onto her feet—to perfectly fit the smooth glass to her toes, her arches, and her heels—God has perfectly fitted you to your purpose. You are the only one prepared for the destiny God has crafted just for you. And you can begin now *putting on* your princess costume every day and behaving like a child of the King.

When you *put on* the shoes that were only made for you to fill, you tend to see things from a little higher up. You become more aware of your purpose and God's ultimate plan for your life. You need to dress yourself for success so that you might begin to look at yourself differently and walk in the way of the Lord. It is only then that you might one day *arrive* at your best.

Do you remember the part where the Grand Duke went all around the kingdom searching for the one whose foot fit the glass slipper? Think about something for me. Do you think for one moment that Cinderella feared that the slipper the Grand Duke was about to put on her foot would not fit? Can you imagine Cinderella being apprehensive or nervous about putting her foot into that slipper in fear that it would not be a perfect fit? Of course not! Cinderella quickly slid her foot into that slipper with the greatest confidence that it would be a perfect fit.

Why? Because that slipper was made specifically for her—it had to fit! It was her shoe, and she knew it. She was the only woman who could wear it with ease.

And you, princess, are the only one who can fill your shoes in this world. They were made only for you. Put them on, sink into them, put your life in order, and arm yourself against the opposing plan of the enemy. Walk with confidence, with assuredness that God is with you. Put on your best clothes and get ready for success. God is waiting.

ACKNOWLEDGE IT

1. Do you recognize some things that are out of order in your life? Your thoughts? Your actions? Your inconsistent prayers? How will you get them in order?
2. Are there things or people in your life that you need to guard yourself against? What or who seems to be a "boulder" in

your pathway that causes you to stumble? What will you do to clear out your pathway so you can walk easier?

3. What are some of the ways you can walk the walk and talk the talk? What are some of the things you can change or do to portray Christ better to your world?

Bring It to God

Lord, thank You for loving me so much that You have instructed me in Your ways. Help me not only to hear Your words but also to do them! I want to do better—I want to be better—for You. I want to be free! Help me to clear my pathway of all that causes me to stumble. It may not be easy, but with You, I can do anything! I love You so much, and I so desperately want to be free to live and serve You all the days of my life—one day at a time. Amen.

Confess It

I will step into the shoes that were made only for me.

I'm not sure exactly what God has planned for me, but I know it's more than anything I could have imagined myself. And I know that in order to arrive at that purpose, even before I reach it, I must dress myself in preparation for it.

Each day, from this day forward, I will be stepping out in love and in the character of Christ. I will seek God's will in aligning myself with His principles. I will arm myself against the enemy and against any worldly elements that may cause me to stumble.

I will dress myself in His purpose.

I will step into the shoes made only for me.

Who ever asked you to feel?
You were chosen to be a princess!
Now go...
Wash your face...
Get a new attitude...
Put on your clothes...
And go be Cinderella!

CHAPTER 8

"And So Be Cinderella!"

PRINCESS PRINCIPLE #7:
SHOW UP AND FULFILL GOD'S ROLE FOR YOU.

---

*He comforts us in all our troubles so that we
can comfort others.*

~ 2 CORINTHIANS 1:4 NLT

After Tommy's words of rebuke, I went into the bathroom, washed my face, changed my attitude, and put on my clothes.

As I neared the end of the hallway that morning, I shoved the metal door open into the backlot area and walked slowly to the gate where I would turn to enter the stage area. Collecting my thoughts and dismissing my feelings, at least for the moment, I stopped just before going out into the public. Standing behind the brown wooden gate, I took one last brief moment to take a deep breath in …and then out.

> *I smiled my best and biggest smile and glided toward them. It was time to go be Cinderella.*

One last time I uttered the words to myself, "I can do this; I'm a princess." Releasing those words from my lips, I turned and walked around the gate and began to walk toward the waiting crowd. As they yelled, "Cinderella, Cinderella!" I smiled my best and biggest smile and glided toward them. It was time to go be Cinderella.

Upon being hired by Tokyo Disneyland to *be* Cinderella and play the roles of the other Disney Princesses, we were first required to go through training and rehearsals so we could learn our respective shows and routines. At our orientation at Disneyland in Anaheim, California, before heading out to Tokyo, each of us girls and guys (our Princes and Peter Pans) were given a packet that contained our job descriptions and a thorough explanation of the characters we were hired to play. One of the booklets within our packet was entitled *Becoming a Disney Face Character.* This packet spelled out for us in great detail a description of each character and how they were to be portrayed.

For instance, Belle was described to us as smart, intelligent, eighteen years old, a little curious, mature, cool, brave with very quick reactions, and very emotionally strong. We were to act accordingly.

Snow White was quite different. She was described as beautiful, happy, playful, and thoughtful, with soft hands, a melodic voice, and a graceful walk. She was gentle and motherly, loved animals, and loved to dance and take care of the dwarfs. We were instructed to never poke fun at anyone, always organize games like

Duck, Duck, Goose and Hokey Pokey on set with the dwarfs, and to always be playful yet gentle, hugging and smiling at every child.

Cinderella, on the other hand, was described for us as gentle, good-natured, friendly, caring, graceful, and poised. Among other things, we were instructed to dance (more specifically, *waltz* with our Prince if he accompanied us), smile, pose for pictures, and curtsy when being introduced. That is exactly how to *be* Cinderella.

That packet also contained an overview of what it means to have been given the opportunity to be a face character. The introduction letter on the first page of the booklet began with these words: "Walt Disney believed in 'entertaining people and bringing pleasure, particularly laughter, to others.'" And it concluded with these words: "With your help, the special magic of Mickey Mouse and his friends will continue to bring smiles to the young at heart and rekindle that childhood spirit that lives in us all."

The spirit of Disney and all its Cast Members is spelled out with one main objective: to serve others.

The one line that speaks to me every time I read it is this one: "As one that dons the Disney costume, you have the unique experience of becoming someone else; Cinderella, Snow White, Mary Poppins…" And in doing so, I had the opportunity to touch the lives of others—to bring joy and hope to the hearts of others and laughter and smiles to the faces of each and every individual whom I was sent out to meet.

Sounds to me a lot like our job description as a servant of the living God.

THE RESPONSIBILITY OF BEING "PERFECT"

People ask me all the time, "What was it like to be a Disney Princess?" Sometimes I think I disappoint them when I tell them that it wasn't all fun and fantasy. It was my job. Sure it was fun, but more than anything it was a responsibility. To go *be* Cinderella, Snow White, Sleeping Beauty, Belle, and Mary Poppins at work each day, we had responsibilities. We girls woke up as ourselves each day and had to get beyond whatever we might be feeling that would keep us from doing our job to its fullest. We washed our faces and got prepped for each show by putting on our makeup, our wigs, and our costumes. We had to get into the mind-set of our characters, just like an actor would do. And then we went out to perform to perfection the characters we were called to portray. Our duty: to forget about ourselves and be who we were supposed to be. Our objective: to touch the lives of those who were waiting on set for us.

We had to be constantly aware of the character we were portraying. If we were in Cinderella, or "Cindy" as we called her, we had to be poised and graceful. If we were in Belle, we had to be intelligent and confident. If we were in Snow White, or "Snow," we had to be playful and gentle. And if we were in "Poppins" we had to be British. (That one snagged me a few times!)

My point to all this is simple. All of the work we did prior to getting on stage was not for ourselves—it was for others. Everything we did every single day was about serving and touching the lives of other people. That was Disney's main focus—others. And it, too, is to be our focus as Christians.

As princesses, we weren't hired to be a perfect model of grace that just stood afar off so others could adore us. Nor were we hired to be lifeless statues or mannequins that got dressed up and set out before the people to be stared at and admired. We were called to *be* someone who would get out there and interact with the people who were waiting on us. We were called to be tangible—to touch them, talk with them, smile at them, and love on them just as they were. We were called to *be* real-life princesses, tangible and human.

And that's what we are called to be as servants of the Lord. We are not called to be perfect models of grace and poise who can no longer relate to the outside world. Nor are we called to be lifeless statues or mannequins to be set out to pose before people as a mere example of how to stand. We are not called to be unapproachable and to stand afar off with judgment and contempt; instead, we are called to get out there, to where they are, to be touchable and tangible as Christ was. We are called to positively affect those who are waiting on us—to give them real answers to life's

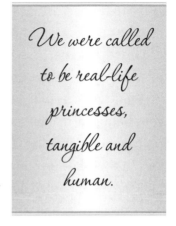

We were called to be real-life princesses, tangible and human.

real questions. To help them to understand that there are real, black-and-white answers to life's most frequently asked questions and to show them the way to live life to its fullest (while we, too, discover its path one step at a time). We are called to love them when they're unlovable as we once were (and sometimes still are) and to accept them just as they are.

That's the model that Jesus gave to us.

We are called to *be* Christians, which means that we are called to be like Him: loving, real, approachable, touchable—and human ...with the scars to prove it.

But Princesses Aren't Supposed to Have Scars

Playing the princess roles in Tokyo were six to eight of us girls who rotated in and out of those costumes each week. One of the reasons we were all chosen was because we all had similar facial features that would keep us all looking like the same girl. To see us each in street clothes, we certainly had our differences, but the goal was that—at least in costume—none of us would have any distinguishing features, scars, or marks that would cause us to be easily told apart.

The challenge for me was that I had a very telling facial scar that screamed, "Same costume, different girl!" That's one huge reason I was always amazed that they had chosen me as a face character.

I got the scar when I was just three years old. My siblings and I were being babysat at a neighbor's house while my parents went out to dinner one evening. The family that was watching us had two pet dogs in their home; one was a very large German shepherd/Labrador retriever mix named Drambui. The other dog was a small poodle that apparently had a bad habit of trying to steal Drambui's food from underneath his belly as he ate. Most of the time, Drambui tolerated the poodle's annoying behavior, but would occasionally snap at him when he was not in the mood. I unfortunately wasn't aware of that behavior at the time.

That night, after the owners went over to feed Drambui, I came along behind them and decided to help. For some strange reason, I thought that Drambui needed someone to hand-feed him—from underneath his belly! So I decided to crawl beneath the large, hungry dog and hand-feed his food up to him. And thinking I was the poodle, Drambui's open jaws came down on my upturned face, burying bottom teeth in my lip and his upper teeth in my forehead. My entire face was literally in his mouth. As a result, my forehead required seventy-five stitches with another ten in my lip, leaving me with a very large scar above my right eye.

The funny thing is, my scar is shaped like a question mark—as if to remind me that I was *clueless* to have attempted to hand-feed a dog that was big enough to be ridden like a horse! But in the long run I was fine; by the grace of God, his teeth stopped just short of reaching my eye. I eventually healed up perfectly and have had no other issues to speak of from the incident, not even a fear of dogs. (I actually went over to play with Drambui when I was released from the hospital.)

The only thing that was really ever affected was how I viewed my own reflection. From that point on, my scar was always the first thing I saw when I looked in a mirror, even though most people never even seemed to notice it. My entire life I have tried to conceal that scar either by makeup or by way of styling my hair to cover it, especially during my time at Disney.

I was constantly reminded that princesses aren't supposed to have scars.

Knowing full well that *princesses aren't supposed to have any scars*, the cosmetology staff was careful to design my wigs expressly so that my scar was hidden at all times. And I was equally as careful to keep it covered. I was constantly reminded that princesses aren't supposed to have scars.

Or are they?

A LESSON ON THE PURPOSE OF SCARS

Believe it or not, over the course of our contracts, each of us girls came to attract fans who would write us fan letters, try to find our houses in the village, and send us presents. Because our fans were annual pass holders, they would come into the park several times a week. I had two fans who went out of their way to come see me when I was on set, to talk with me, take photos with me, and try to communicate with me.

Although it was prohibited, they knew how to get in contact with us at home, and provided that they weren't "strange, obsessed" fans, most of us girls had no issue with making friends with them. My fans and I became close friends, and for my birthday, they and several of my wardrobe staff friends came over to celebrate with me. As we sat around my living room talking, I inquired of one woman why, as a fan, she had chosen me, out of all the other girls. I knew I wasn't the prettiest or the most believable. So I wondered why she felt so drawn toward *me*.

"We all look the same, don't we?" I asked.

With that question, she smiled and began to explain through broken English that one day when I was out in the park as Cinderella, she came up to take a picture with me. As I looked over toward her, she said a big gust of wind parted the bangs of my wig, and she saw my scar. Then looking up at my forehead, she pointed to the scar on my forehead and she continued, "And *that's* why I liked you. When I saw your scar I knew…you were just like me."

GOD'S PERSPECTIVE ON SCARS

For the first time in my life, I saw my scars differently. And then later in life, once I came into my relationship with Christ, God had to remind me of that incident to show me that it was that scar, the one I spent my life trying to hide, that caused her to feel connected to me on a different level. You see, when she came up to me while I was in costume, she was in awe of me as an actress portraying her favorite character. But then she saw my humanity. She saw that I, too, was flawed—as she apparently was. She could relate to me even though I was standing in the shoes that she would never have the opportunity to fill.

It was that scar—that I had always been so ashamed to show— that caused her to notice that I *was* different all right, but not in the way I had always felt. It made me different in a good way. In my role as a princess, it made me human, touchable, and accessible. And it spoke to her in a way my words couldn't. It told the story that I, like her, even as an actress playing a role that she would have loved to play, had some hurts and wounds in my life that needed healing too. My scar told her that I was just like her. My scar spoke to her that day.

Jesus' scars do the same for Him. Have you ever wondered why God had the ability to raise His Son, Jesus, from the dead, yet He never bothered to remove the scars? Maybe those scars serve a great purpose. The scars on His hands, His feet, His side, and His back all tell the story of His crucifixion for our sins. They remind us of what He endured. They prove to us that He is real, that He was human just like us, fighting the fight of faith in this world. And His scars were left there to tell us that He was wounded as we are wounded but that His Father—our Father—has the ability to bind up wounds and heal those hurts left by the cruelty of this world.

> *Ever wonder why God had the ability to raise Jesus from the dead, yet He never bothered to remove the scars?*

His scars spoke to Thomas to testify of where He had been. And His nail-scarred hands served as proof to His disciples that He truly was who He proclaimed Himself to be to the Samaritan woman. Jesus' scars still speak to us today.

God wants to use your scars as well...

SCARS: THE GREATEST STORYTELLERS OF ALL

We've spent a great deal of time going back to our pasts, exposing wounds, and learning how to heal them once and for all. We spent time getting new attitudes, changing our way of thinking, and putting on a new character. And we did this for good reason. It wasn't just so that you could be healed, free, and able to enjoy life to its fullest—although it does please God to see His children loving the life He gave us (see Gal. 5:1).

But the big reason—are you ready?—was so that you could get over yourself long enough to realize that this life isn't about you… and it's not about me either. These steps and principles were never about just getting us cleaned up, healed up, and dressed up so we can stand as a perfect model for others to admire. It has always been about us getting cleaned up, healed up, and dressed up in our new character so that we can go out to where others are and reach them for Jesus.

God had you go back to the past so that you could see that your gaping, oozing wounds, when cleaned and healed properly, leave scars—scars that tell your story and speak to the world. Scars are conversation pieces, and they are great storytellers. Scars tell a *story* of the event that caused the wound and the pain that was once there. But the scars also speak of their *healer.* They even prompt people to *ask* you what happened so that you can then tell them your story.

You see, God wants us now to take a huge faith-filled step farther. He wants us to use our past to minister to someone else's future. We do this by simply telling our story. Your story likely rests in the place where you have felt the most pain, which is why it was so important for those areas to be recognized and healed up. Your story is likely found in the place where your greatest wounds were inflicted and the biggest scar remains. The world needs your story, and if you plan to remain fulfilled in this life, then you will need to discover your purpose by sharing it. Your story is the place where your pain *becomes* your purpose, your heartache *becomes* your heartbeat to reach others, and your former misery *becomes* your opportunity for ministry.

Your story can be found right here, where your old intersects your new. It's the place of your testimony. *Testimony* means proof—proof of God. Just as a scar is proof that there was once a painful wound, so, too, is your story, or your testimony, proof to a dying world that you were once where they are now. It is because of where you've been that you can now know with certainty where you're going.

> God wants us to use our past to minister to someone else's future.

Jesus confidently said in John 8:14, "For I know where I came from and where I am going." It is nothing to be ashamed of.

It is *your* story and *your* scars that will testify now of God's love, healing, and grace far better than anything you will ever find to reach this world for Jesus.

A Model for All Time

We see a perfect model for showing our scars and telling our own stories in the woman at the well. She was the Samaritan woman looking for love and acceptance in all the wrong places—married five times, living with her sixth man, running from the world, and desperately seeking purpose for her life. (See John chapter 4.)

What we haven't yet explored about this woman was *why* Jesus went out of His way to go where Jews were not even supposed to go, to meet with a woman with a bad reputation, only to slice open the wounds of her past. Why did He go through the trouble? And why did He deal with her so harshly as to immediately dig up her past and touch on her painful wounds? And why did He deem her so worthy to have chosen *her* as the very first person that He ever revealed Himself to as the Messiah?

He had a great purpose for her life. She didn't yet know it, but God had destined her to be a great woman of faith who would go on to be one of the greatest evangelists of her time.

Let's look closer at her story to see what came of her life after meeting with Jesus.

THE GREATEST NOBODY I NEVER KNEW

I like to refer to the woman at the well as the greatest nobody I never knew. I would have loved to meet her. I think we would have been fast friends (provided she and I had already read this book and gotten over our own self-issues first!)

From her story in John 4, she seems to have been a loner, prone to avoid conflict, and most likely sick and tired of being talked about, which, as we mentioned earlier, may be why she was at the well at such an odd hour. She was probably very beautiful as well, which I'm sure didn't help to cultivate female friendships. She was never given a physical description, but seeing that she had been married five times, and she was on her sixth man, she couldn't have been dog ugly! Her track record also indicates that she was probably prone to neediness when it came to the attention and affection of men.

One of the most interesting things about this woman is that she was never given a name. Though Jesus went out of His way to meet with her and thought her important enough to entrust her with His secret that He was in fact the Savior of the world, He never actually called her by name. To this day, we only refer to her as "the Samaritan woman" or "the woman at the well" because we have no other name for her. I always thought that was sad, but then I suppose she really didn't need a name. She had already had five, and none of them were working for her! What I suppose she really needed was a purpose. And that's exactly what she received that day.

Jesus thought this wounded woman with a bad reputation to be so important and her purpose to be so valuable that He went there, purposefully, to that obscure place in Samaria where Jews normally would have no business being, to talk to someone a Jew would ordinarily never speak to, and reveal Himself to her. You see, Jesus had good reason for this divine appointment. He had gone to Samaria to reap a harvest of souls and to impact the lives of the Samaritan people (see John 4:35, 38). But He didn't go there to preach to the Samaritan people Himself; He went there to meet with the woman who would go out and do it for Him.

And did she ever.

After meeting with Jesus, the disciples arrived back to the well where she and Jesus were speaking. Upon their arrival, she ran off back into the very city that shunned her to tell the people about the man she had just met and her own story as well. " 'Come see a man who knew all about the things I did, who knows me inside and out. Do you think this could be the Messiah?' And they went out to see for themselves" (John 4:29 MSG).

And that's how the kingdom of God works: Jesus reveals Himself to us, we go out and reveal Him to the world, and others come see for themselves. And the cycle continues.

It's just that simple.

That's why she was considered one of the greatest evangelists of her time. She did what you and I are supposed to be doing. She had an encounter with Jesus, and she immediately went to tell others about Him. She got healed and went about leading others to the Healer. She got over herself and beyond her issues, and she went out to help others do the same.

She didn't wait to go to seminary or to know the Word of God forward and backward, inside and out. She didn't wait to see if she felt led to do something great for God. She just discovered the will of God for her life—to share hope with others. And she just did it! She went out, taking only what she had been equipped with—zeal, excitement, and most importantly her story—and she changed her world with it!

And that is precisely what we are now called to do. Take our freedom and the comfort we have received from God throughout this process and go impact our world!

> *He comforts us in all our troubles so that we can comfort others. When they are troubled, we will be able to give them the same comfort God has given us.*
>
> ~ 2 CORINTHIANS 1:4 NLT

Our stories are invaluable to the mission of sharing God's love with others just as it was with the woman at the well. John 4:39–42 tells us:

> Many Samaritans from the village believed in Jesus because the woman had said, *"He told me everything I ever did!"* When they came out to see him, they begged him to stay in their village. So he stayed for two days, long enough for many more to hear his message and believe. Then they said to the woman, "Now we believe, not just because of what you told us, but because we have heard him ourselves. *Now we know that he is indeed the Savior of the world"* (NLT, emphasis mine).

You see, before they ever laid eyes on Jesus Himself, they listened to the words of a woman whom they had known, and known well. They not only knew her, but they had seen (and probably whispered about) the very wounds that caused her shame. This time, when she returned from one of her visits to the far-off well, she came back not with wounds but with scars and a story of how those wounds were healed—by unconditional love and acceptance from a stranger. She was delivered of the pain, and she no longer walked in shame. This time, she came boldly to the village and looked each one of those people square in the eye—something she had not done in quite some time. It was her story, her testimony that led them all to Jesus.

> *Our stories are invaluable to the mission of sharing God's love with others.*

FINDING YOUR STORY

I believe wholeheartedly that one of the most powerful tools in your arsenal to reaching the hurting world around you is your story. Why? Because no one can ever argue with your story. They may be able to debate theology, doctrine or your scriptural interpretations, but no one stands a chance against the power of your own personal story! I often say: your story is found in the place where your "old" intersects your "new". Its the story of that moment when God saw you in need, came to you, reached out His hand to you, then picked you up, brushed you off, and wrapped His unconditional love and acceptance around you. It's that story that holds the power to penetrate the hardest of hearts and instill hope into the most unbelieving of cynics. It's the story you must find. The story you must use. And the story you must never get too "holy" to tell.

You see, God intends for us to use our pasts to minister to someone else's future. He wants us to go out into our communities and share our stories. He calls us to be tangible, to be real, and to offer them hope by sharing with them our testimonies of His grace.

Don't Let Shame Shut You Up!

If you are reading this and the one thing that is going through your mind is, *There's no way I could ever share what I have been through with another human being!* then I challenge you to examine whether it is shame that is keeping you silent. If you're struggling about sharing your experience with someone who needs to hear it or you're too ashamed to testify about a struggle God delivered you from in the past, then there are two Scriptures I want you to receive into your heart. One is found in Hebrews 2:9, and the other is found in Hebrews 2:18. Both of them changed my life and set me completely free!

Hebrews 2:9 says this: "But we see Jesus, who was made a little lower than the angels, now crowned with glory and honor because he suffered death, *so that by the grace of God he might taste death for everyone*" (emphasis mine).

And Hebrews 2:18: "*Because* he himself suffered when *he was tempted, he is able to help those who are being tempted*" (emphasis mine).

In both of these verses, we see that for Jesus (and for us) there is a purpose for the pain and temptation that we have been allowed to walk through in

> There is a purpose for the pain and temptation that we have been allowed to walk through.

our lives. These particular verses show us that we endure these things for others—so that we can minister to others from a perspective of someone who has *been there, done that, and understands!* Jesus Himself has lived in this human flesh; He knows what it is to suffer, to taste death and the sting of pain, and to be tempted by the enemy (see Matt. 4). All of it—all the trials of life, the mistakes of yesterday, the sorrows of today, and each and every weakness we have—they all provide us with the common ground on which we can stake our claim to others that God's grace is sufficient in any time of need (see 2 Cor. 12:9). God's strength is made perfect in our weaknesses—so breathe easy.

It is nothing to be ashamed of!

By the Words of Our Testimonies

God never intended for us to carry around the shame that is associated with a sin that He has already forgiven. Jesus died to take both our sin and our shame from us. Shame is the enemy's way of trying to keep us from telling our stories and sharing our freedom with others who need it. God does not want you silenced by your shame. If you endured the death or temptation of sin and it has resulted in shame, give it to God and then ask Him to help you use it for His glory.

One Scripture that helped me so much to overcome the residual shame left after God had forgiven my sins was Revelation 12:11. It simply tells us that we are made overcomers by what Jesus did on the cross two thousand years ago and by the word of our own testimonies today. In other words, if you and I want to be completely free from our past, we

If you want to be free from your past, you must learn to use it against the enemy!

must learn to use it against the enemy! We must be willing not only to accept forgiveness of the sin but to share our testimony of freedom freely and without shame.

Ask God to prepare you to share your story with others. It is important that you know how to communicate your testimony to others. Your testimony is your personal story that focuses on three basic things: what your life was like before you came to know and trust in Christ, how you came to surrender to Him, and the difference in your life since committing yourself to Him. Here's a great outline by Mary Fairchild entitled "How to Write Your Christian Testimony":[1]

- **Before:**
  Simply tell what your life was like before you surrendered to Christ. What were you searching for before coming to know Christ? What was the key problem, emotion, situation, or attitude you were dealing with? What motivated you? What were your actions? How did you try to satisfy your inner needs? (Examples of inner needs are loneliness, fear of death, insecurity. Possible ways to fill those needs include work, money, drugs, relationships, sports, sex.)

- **How:**
  How were you converted? Simply tell the events and circumstances that caused you to consider Christ as the solution to your searching. Take time to identify the steps that brought you to the point of trusting Christ. Where were you? What was happening at the time? What people or problems influenced your decision?

- **Since:**
  How has your life in Christ made a difference? How has His forgiveness impacted you? How have your thoughts, attitudes, and emotions changed? Share how Christ is

meeting your needs and what a relationship with Him means to you now.

Fairchild also offers these tips to remember when giving your testimony:[2]

- **Stick to the point.** Your conversion and new life in Christ should be the main points.
- **Be specific.** Include events, genuine feelings, and personal insights that clarify your main point. This makes your testimony tangible—something others can relate to.
- **Be current.** Tell what is happening in your life with God now, today.
- **Be honest.** Don't exaggerate or dramatize your life for effect. The simple truth of what God has done in your life is all the Holy Spirit needs to convict others of their sin and convince them of His love and grace.

Throughout years of ministry, I've seen a vast number of believers who don't know exactly how to share their testimony and, therefore, are terrified of doing it! Don't worry—God may never require you to stand on a mountaintop to share it with the world, but He does reserve the right to ask you to share it with at least one person whom He knows that you can help. So don't be afraid. Whether it's one-on-one at a coffee shop or speaking to an audience at your church or youth group, there's nothing to fear. You will know who and how and when to share your testimony. God will lead you and put the words in your mouth (see Luke 12:11).

Seek out people who need to hear the things you've been through, or at the very least, keep your eyes open for those God sends your way! This is about more than just sharing your story of salvation. God is going to bring you people who are struggling with issues and things that you, too, have struggled with in the past. You will be required to be open and honest about the pains and shame of your past. But remember, you are only sharing the story of your past pain so you can lead them to the One who can heal them and free them too—it's about Him. Your story will lead them to Him. Get out of the way and let God do the healing. You don't have to have all the answers; you just have to be able to lead them to the One who does!

Knock! At some point, God may lead you to begin finding places where you can use your testimony on a regular basis or as part of a ministry. I believe that is what God expects from us—to find a way in which to reach out and extend the grace that God has extended to us in any way we can!

I believe that the greatest person to ever minister to an alcoholic is someone who's been an alcoholic. The best rape counselor is someone who's been raped. The best one to ever minister to a brokenhearted mother is one who's been brokenhearted and made whole again. The greatest person to ever minister to the millions of girls every year who are having abortions is the Christian woman who is now free of the pain and the shame of having one herself.

Some of the greatest ministries were birthed out of the worst personal failures and mistakes. I know many women today who are now ministry directors in centers for abortive mothers or unwed mothers because they themselves have stood in those same shoes and are no longer ashamed to share it. Many abuse victims have gotten healing for themselves and have gone on to be counselors in that same field because they know what it's like to be there.

This is the will of God, plain and simple—to reach out to a hurting world.

Ask God if you are called into an area where you once struggled. If so, seek out where your testimony can be used and knock. The worst they can say is, "no." And if so, find another door to knock on.

There are literally hundreds of ways that we can reach out to those who are where we have been. This is the will of God, plain and simple—to reach out to a hurting world (starting with those who are right there in our own home), to be Christlike, touching lives and effecting change in this world. We can start by reaching into the lives of those who are nearest and dearest to us. Then we can look out and reach out beyond the four walls of our own homes. You can begin by recognizing whether God has given you a "soft spot" for someone or something specific. Perhaps you feel drawn to or especially compassionate towards babies, children, families in need, addicts, the incarcerated, unwed mothers, the abandoned, the abused, the elderly, the shut-ins, the handicapped, the poor, the hungry, needy people, homeless people, hurting people, athletes, students, teens, divorcées, single parents, parents who have lost children, or spouses who have lost their loved ones…

If you'll just take notice of what "pulls on your heart-strings," you may discover a need that God is calling you to fill. And here's the neatest part about giving: according to John 4:34, it is in that place of giving of yourself to accomplish God's will on earth that we actually find the most fulfillment in life! How great is that? God makes it so that, when we give out, we actually experience a joy that fills us up like nothing else ever could! So look around! The possibilities are endless. Find a local charity or Christian church or ministry that could use your story, your gifting, or your helping hands. And if you don't have the time or the physical ability to help personally, then give financially to a ministry that is sharing the Gospel with others or that is working with those you feel called to help. And if you don't have the money, then dig into your closets and find some resources that could be used to aid those who are working in an area of ministry that you feel led to support.

Imagine a world where we all reached out to give of our time, our efforts, our money, or our resources.

Imagine the good we could do if we looked into ourselves and instead of seeing all that we can't do or all that we don't have, we were able to look in and see some of the awesome giftings and abilities that God has given us to benefit others.

Every one of us has something we're good at and something we could give. And if we look into our hearts, we all have *some* idea of where we'd like to reach out and make a difference!

Sometimes it's just a simple smile or a word of encouragement at a grocery store to a clerk who looks like she's lost her best friend. It doesn't always have to be difficult and time consuming. We just have to look beyond ourselves long enough to see the needs of others.

We must be willing to ask God how He wants us to do it and then follow His lead.

God will always find a way to use a willing vessel!

TELLING YOUR STORY

I've been told by well-meaning Christians that I shouldn't talk about my past, that it brings glory to the enemy. To that I would wholeheartedly and adamantly disagree. I imagine the enemy would love nothing more than for all of us to keep our stories silenced by that lie.

> *We have to look beyond ourselves long enough to see the needs of others.*

There has never been a time that I have shared the story of my former life without following it up with Jesus' story, the story of the cross. Since I've gotten over myself, I have never minded showing my scars because it always opened up an opportunity to share about the One who healed me.

You see, I know the difference between what I had done and who I am now in Christ, so it doesn't bother me a bit to refer to that old person or the sinful things she used to do.

Now, I'm not stupid. I never divulge the names of those who have wounded me or tell stories about someone who would be hurt by my telling it. And I don't share the gory details of my sin. I simply couple some God-given wisdom with my transparency, and as a result, I find that God opens up platforms for me to talk about the real-life issues that need to be addressed.

Don't ever allow the enemy or anyone else to tell you that you should never speak of your past after you get healed of it. God never intended for us to forget our pasts; He intends for us to be *forgiven* of our past sins, and then use that as our present proof to a lost and dying world that needs His forgiveness too. He is our Redeemer. He takes the dreadful past and redeems it, or exchanges it, for a glorious future. If He intended for us to forget the past, He would have also erased our memory of it when He forgave us, just as He would have healed us without scars if He wanted us to forget about what happened there. We should use the memory of our pasts to remind us of where we have come from and how we never intend to go back. And we should use those scars from old wounds to remind others of God's healing power. We must always remember that there are people out there who are going through what we have gone through and feeling what we have felt, and God wants to send us to them. We can use our pasts to help us identify with those who are hurting as we once hurt, and dying as we once were.

I believe that we must learn to get real and identify with the world if we ever expect them to listen to what we have to say. As the church, we must be careful to never get too "holy" that we stop telling our stories. We cannot continue to pretend like we have it all together or that we have never been as vile as others feel themselves to be. We have to become real to an unbelieving world. We must show up with our scars just as Jesus had to do for doubting Thomas before He ascended into heaven. Like the woman at the well, we, too, can lead them to Jesus with our stories. We can bring purpose to our pain, and from it the misery of our lives can become ministry for the Lord.

It is in yesterday where we find our purpose for today.

I have been forgiven, and those open wounds that came from sin and shame have now been healed over. But thankfully, I still have the scars to prove it. I have determined that I shall not hide them. Rather, I choose to let my scars speak, giving testimony to who Christ says He is—my Healer, my Deliverer, my Everything!

As the saying goes: *God never wastes a hurt!* Your past will serve a wonderful purpose if we'll let it. This is what it means to allow God to turn your pain into purpose, your misery into ministry, and your heartaches into your heartbeats.

That's what God wants to do in all of our lives!

KEEPING PERSPECTIVE THROUGH THE PAIN

When we go through periods of death in our lives, times of depression, divorce, abuse, financial trouble, loss, and hurt, we must remember to walk through them by the grace of God and be encouraged that God is simply equipping us for His service.

James 1:2–4 says, "Consider it a sheer gift, friends, when tests and challenges come at you from all sides. You know that under pressure, your faith-life is forced into the open and shows its true colors. So don't try to get out of anything prematurely. Let it do its work so you become mature and well-developed, not deficient in any way" (MSG).

As we journey, God's grace will see us through and sustain us in the process (see 2 Cor. 12:9). And when we finally get to the other side of it, we will be proof, a testament to a hurting world, that God is who He says He is! Someone is watching you go through it all, and it is telling your story—His story. Keep your perspective and stay focused on this truth: God always has a plan—even if that plan is nothing more than to teach you His ways.

He can turn the bad around for good (see Rom. 8:28) and help us to see that though we may not be able to change yesterday, we can choose to learn from it and to use it to help others. For it is in yesterday where we find our purpose for today.

Acknowlege It

1. Have you been one who is guilty of hiding her scars? Why? Has the enemy convinced you to keep silent lest someone think less of you?

2. What are some of the issues and mistakes that you have learned the most from? Can you see how you can use them now to glorify God? What are they? And is there someone you can think of who needs to hear where you've been so they, too, can learn of God's grace for their own lives?

3. What is your personal testimony? Have you sat down and taken inventory of all God has brought you through and the life lessons He has taught you? Sit down and jot it all down.

Be prepared. God may just be waiting to send you someone to share it with!

Bring It to God

Lord, thank You for all You have taught me through this book, and thank You for all You have taught me and brought me through in this life.

I am so relieved and encouraged to know that it is not all wasted! It all had a greater purpose—one that I am realizing now. Help me, Lord, to see the bigger picture—that life isn't always about me! Help me to get over myself once and for all so I can see all that You have for me to accomplish for You from day to day!

Send me to those who need me and my story. And when they're right in front of me, help me not to be afraid to reach out to meet their needs. Help me, Lord, to share my story and to show my scars. I know now that they are nothing to be ashamed of!

I am so grateful to You for all You are and all that You've done in me.

I love You, Lord.

Amen.

Confess It

I will show up and fulfill God's role for me.

I've been selfish and self-absorbed. I've neglected my role in impacting others by concentrating solely on myself.

But that is the past. Now begins my future.

I have all I need.

I am walking in faith. I was chosen. I've gone back. I'm healed up, washed off, and I have a brand-new attitude for life. I am dressed in His perfection and am now wearing my purpose. I am called to be who God has always destined me to be.

From this point on, I will not wait to feel. I will make no excuses. I will show up.

I know that God has prepared an amazing role for me and has perfectly equipped me to fulfill it. I just have to trust His plan.

I'm over myself. I am here to serve others in His name.

I am prepared.

I am ready.

I will go.

Who's Waiting on You?

What I haven't told you yet is the way my day ended after Tommy instructed me to get back to work. I had no idea that by the end of that day, my dysfunctional fairy tale would end and the rest of my life would begin. What happened that day has now become my heartbeat and my purpose. It has become my ministry.

Just as I rounded the gate and glided out as Cinderella into a sea of screaming fans and guests, I was intercepted by my captain. My "character captain" accompanied me on my meet-and-greet sets to be sure I got in and out on time and to help me should I have need of anything while out there among the people.

As my captain walked toward me, I was afraid that I had done something wrong. I thought the worst, but then found that what he was about to tell me was even worse than I had expected. Only this time, it wasn't about me.

> *I had no idea that by the end of that day, my dysfunctional fairy tale would end and the rest of my life would begin.*

Pulling me aside, he told me that there was a family in the park that had come especially to see me. Glancing over his shoulder as I listened, I saw a family with two children—a boy and a girl who looked to be about seven to ten years old—sitting quietly off to the side away from the crowd. Looking more closely, I could see that both children had braces on their legs. I wondered if I was ready for them that day.

As my captain continued, he told me that the family had been waiting patiently in the park for me all morning. He went on to explain that the little boy was terminally ill and that his last wish was simply to meet me and maybe spend some time with me.

Once again, I breathed a deep breath and then started toward the family. The smiles on their faces told me that meeting Cinderella in person was truly a dream come true. They obviously didn't know the person behind my costume. All I could think about was that here was this little boy, waiting on me, believing in me, and yet it was all I could do to get over myself long enough to show up and make a small difference in this family's life.

As I walked up to the family, my eyes began to fill with tears. Then, being mindful of the part I was called to play, I managed to dry my tears and refocus on what I had to do.

My captain served as my interpreter as we tried our best to communicate about nothing. They were shy, and I was broken, so it was best that our hearts did all the talking. I spent the next twenty-five minutes of my set visiting with him and his family, signing autographs, and posing for pictures.

Everything inside of me withered with the fear that they would see me—the real me—in those photographs. I didn't want to disappoint him as I felt I had with everyone else in my life. So I silently prayed that this little boy would not see me for who I really was: broken, miserable, and dying on the inside. *Instead, God, please let him see…You!*

I believe he did.

Just as our time together was ending, he spoke whispered words into the ear of my captain. My captain interpreted, "Cinderella, when you get on top of your really big float, would you look for me?"

Knowing just how difficult it would be to find one child out of the tens of thousands of children and families along the parade route, I bent down on one knee, put my gloved hands in his hands, and said confidently, "Yes, I will find you!"

And as I said my goodbyes and turned to walk away, a thought came to my mind: *What if I hadn't shown up today?*

The instant that God had me revisit that particular moment in time, my life gained a whole new meaning. I knew it could no longer be about me, my issues, my feelings, my difficulties. I finally understood that when He had instructed me to "get over myself," it was because He loved me; He wanted to fill me with purpose and help me to fulfill my destiny. It was now about everyone else—everyone He had placed in my life. I realized instantly that the way I lived my life really *did* have an impact on the world around me. Even on terminally ill children I had never before met.

I also realized that there is not one of us on this planet whose life does not matter to someone. We all have someone who is waiting on us.

So let me ask *you* now, princess…

Who Is Waiting on You?

Throughout this book I have had the privilege of opening my heart to you to expose some of the same aches, pains, and misconceptions that I myself have had to overcome. I have identified the wounds of my life so that I could then share with you how God healed them and created scars that speak, sharing my story of redemption and restoration with you. I am honored to be able to share it with you. But the fact of the matter is: It is *your* story that matters now.

Someone is waiting on *you*.

Someone is waiting on you.

Jesus went to the well that day to deliver to the Samaritan woman the purpose she had been searching for all her life. But before He could deliver it to her, He needed to make her whole so that He then could send her into a broken world.

And that is exactly what He has done for you throughout this book. He has been making you whole.

He did all of this—bringing you through the steps and principles of this book—because somebody right now is waiting on you, on your story, on your testimony of a healing God who cares about their brokenness.

You can lead them to Jesus with your story. And with it, you can bring purpose to your own pain; and from it, the misery of your own life can become a ministry for your God that will fulfill you like nothing ever could.

We never know what purpose God may have lined up for us. We don't know who or what is around the corner, just waiting for us to show up and be ourselves. As we've learned from David, Esther, Aaron, and Ruth, despite the circumstances that are staring us in the face, it *is* possible to get up and get over ourselves so that we, too, can discover that there is someone waiting on us.

God has given you everything you need—genetics, experience, geographic location. His Word, His guidance, His love.

What are you waiting for?

Later that afternoon, I climbed high onto the top of my float, determined to find my little friend. For the first time in a long time, I boarded my float with a deep sense of purpose. As I started down the parade route, I chose to focus only on finding him—the one person whom I knew believed in me, instead of all the ones who looked as though they didn't.

It was also in that very moment that I found some much-needed perspective.

About midway through the parade, in the midst of an ocean of unfamiliar faces, I finally found him—smiling, waving, and frantically blowing me kisses. It was also in that very moment that I found some much-needed perspective.

I know now that I was not there for that child that day; he was there for me. He was there to remind me that God can use anyone to touch a life. I understood that there was a bigger picture to be seen, but it could only be seen from His perspective. Someone was waiting on me that day, and I'm glad he was. I realized that there will always be somebody, somewhere, who is waiting on me just as there will always be somebody, somewhere, who is waiting on *you*.

Nearly every day of my life, especially on the days that I get too caught up in myself or my feelings, I think of that little boy and I intentionally ask myself, *Who's waiting on me to show up while I am waiting to feel?*

Perhaps you should do the same.

Regardless of your problems or your past, you have been given all you need to recover from your issues and step into your destiny.

Pull yourself up off the floor and just show up. He will do the rest. Regardless of your feelings, square your shoulders, put on your purpose, and remind yourself that you were chosen—specifically chosen for such a time as this (see Esther 4:14).

You were chosen—specifically chosen for such a time as this.

Turn it over to God, and let Him lead your way.

Besides, "Who ever asked you to feel? You were chosen to be a princess! Now go, wash your face, get a new attitude, put on your clothes, and go be Cinderella!"

You'll be amazed at who's waiting on you.

Endnotes

Chapter 2

1. Dr. Caroline Leaf, *Who Switched Off My Brain?: Controlling Toxic Thoughts and Emotions* p.19-20 (n.p.: Switch on Your Brain USA Inc., 2008).

2. James Strong, *The New Strong's Exhaustive Concordance of the Bible: Dictionary of the Hebrew Bible Dictionary of the Greek Testament* (Nashville: Thomas Nelson, 1996).

3. Dr. Caroline Leaf, *Who Switched Off My Brain?: Controlling Toxic Thoughts and Emotions* (Switch on Your Brain USA Inc., 2008).

4. Rick Warren, *The Purpose Driven Life* (Grand Rapids: Zondervan, 2002), 182.

5. Pam Stenzel, *Sex, Love & Relationships Curriculum*, DVD (Vision Video Inc., 1998).

Chapter 3

1. Bill Gothard and the Institute in Basic Life Principles, www.iblp.com.

2. Bill Gothard, "What I Teach," The Institute in Basic Life Principles, http://billgothard.com/bill/about/whatiteach/

3. Nick Vujicic, "About Nick Vujicic," Life without Limbs, http://www.life withoutlimbs.org/about-nick-vujicic.php

4. Ibid.

5. Ibid.

Chapter 5

1. Paula White, *Deal with It!: You Cannot Conquer What You Will Not Confront* (Nashville: Thomas Nelson, 2004), 109.

2. "mourn," Dictionary.com, *Dictionary.com Unabridged (v 1.1)*, Random House, Inc., http://dictionary.reference.com/browse/mourn

3. Frank Minirth and Paul Meier, *Happiness Is a Choice: The Symptoms, Causes, and Cures of Depression*, Revised ed. p.39 (Grand Rapids: Baker Books, 1994).

4. Ibid.

5. Making a Habit of Success, by Mack R. Douglas, Galahad Books, a division of BBS Publishing Corp, New York, New York. (Published by arrangement with Pelican Publishing Company, Inc.) copyright 1999. p.241 (ISBN: 1-57866-071-8)

6. Frank Minirth and and Paul Meier, *Happiness is a Choice: The Symptoms, Causes, and Cures of Depression*, Revised ed. (Grand Rapids: Baker Books, 1994), pp 16, 52

7. "Quotations," www.thinkexist.com

Chapter 6

1. Blue Letter Bible, "Dictionary and Word Search for *mashach (Strong's 4886)*," Blue Letter Bible (1996–2009), http://www.blueletterbible.org/lang/lexicon/lexicon.cfm?strongs=H4886

2. Blue Letter Bible, "Dictionary and Word Search for *cuwk (Strong's 5480)*," Blue Letter Bible (1996–2009), http://www.blueletterbible.org/lang/lexicon/lexicon.cfm?strongs=H5480

3. Rick Warren, *The Purpose Driven Church: Growth without Compromising Your Message & Mission* p.352 (Grand Rapids: Zondervan, 1995).

4. A. W. Tozer *The Knowledge of the Holy* p.viii (New York: HarperOne, 1978)

5. Ibid.

6. Dr. Caroline Leaf, *Who Switched Off My Brain?: Controlling Toxic Thoughts and Emotions* p.20 (Switch on Your Brain USA Inc., 2008).

7. John Baker, *Life's Healing Choices: Freedom from Your Hurts, Hang-ups, and Habits* (New York: Howard Books, 2007), 140–141.

8. Blue Letter Bible, "Dictionary and Word Search for *ginosko (Strong's 1097)*," Blue Letter Bible (1996–2009), http://www.blueletterbible.org/lang/lexicon/lexicon.cfm?strongs=G1097

9. Blue Letter Bible, "Dictionary and Word Search for *yada` (Strong's 3045)*," Blue Letter Bible (1996–2009), http://www.blueletterbible.org/lang/lexicon/lexicon.cfm?strongs=H3045

Chapter 7

1. James Strong, *The New Strong's Exhaustive Concordance of the Bible: Dictionary of the Hebrew Bible Dictionary of the Greek Testament* (Nashville: Thomas Nelson, 1996).

Chapter 8

1. Mary Fairchild, "How to Write Your Christian Testimony: 6 Easy Steps for Putting Together Your Christian Testimony," About.com, http://christianity.about.com/od /testimonies/a/howtotestimony.htm
2. Ibid.

Recommended Reading

Dear friend,

As promised, here is a short list of some wonderfully insightful books (in no particular order) that have particularly helped me in my quest to get over myself, my past, and my issues. This is by no means an exhaustive list. I merely wish to provide some additional support for your journey and to reinforce the fact that freedom is anything but free—it takes time, effort, energy, consistency, and determination to get free and stay free of the issues that would want to keep us bound and unable to enjoy our everyday lives. I pray God's richest blessings be upon you as you continue to grow in faith and in knowledge of our God and His precious Word. And may you always remember that each and every day, somebody somewhere is waiting on YOU!

- *Happiness is a Choice* by Frank Minirth, M.D and Paul Meier, M.D.
- *The Christian Atheist* by Craig Groeschel
- *You are Not What You Weigh* by Lisa Bevere
- *Why You Do What You Do* by Bobb Biehl
- *Who Switched Off My Brain* by Dr. Caroline Leaf
- *Life's Healing Choices* by John Baker
- *Kissed the Girls and Made Them Cry* by Lisa Bevere
- *How to Succeed at Being Yourself* by Joyce Meyer
- *Breaking Free* by Beth Moore

- All three books: *Cut, Violated* and *Starved* by Nancy Alcorn of Mercy Ministries
- Any and all of John Maxwell's books on leadership and personal growth
- *Deal with It!* by Paula White
- *Managing Your Emotions* by Joyce Meyer
- *Fasting* by Jentezen Franklin
- *For Women Only* by Shaunti Feldhahn
- *Power Thoughts* by Joyce Meyer
- *Every Woman's Battle* by Shannon Ethridge and Stephen Arterburn
- *The Costly Anointing* by Lori Wilke
- *Fear Fighters* by Jentezen Franklin
- *Where is God* by Dr. John Townsend

About Jennifer

Jennifer Beckham is a wife, mother, author, evangelist, Bible teacher, and the founder of Jennifer Beckham Ministries. For over a decade, Jennifer has traveled the United States and Canada sharing her powerful testimony, preaching the life-giving truths of God's Word, and teaching practical, biblical principles to thousands in churches and conference centers.

In addition to her ministry to women and churches, Jennifer serves as a motivational speaker for corporate events and secular organizations. She also serves as a "character educator" for the public school system integrating positive values into students and speaking candidly to teens about real-life issues such as drug abuse, promiscuity, eating disorders, cutting, and low self-worth. To date, Jennifer has had the wonderful privilege of speaking into the lives of more than 400,000 students in over 450 public schools through-out the U.S. and Canada.

Jennifer has appeared as a featured guest on several television broadcasts including Daystar's *Celebration* with Marcus and Joni Lamb, *Life Today* with James and Betty Robison, *100 Huntley Street* in Canada, and *The Paula Today Show* with Paula White.

A native Floridian, Jennifer lives in Jacksonville, Florida with her husband and fellow minister, Anthony, and their two beautiful children, Cole and Jordan Paige.

To learn more about Jennifer or to contact her or her ministry, please visit

www.JenniferBeckham.org

About Jennifer Beckham Ministries

Jennifer Beckham Ministries (JBM) exists to impact the world with the message of hope, freedom, and love through Jesus Christ. Through conferences and events, media, and the development and distribution of practical teaching resources, we are challenging and equipping women of all ages to grow their faith beyond mere inspiration onto a level of true transformation.

At JBM, it is our mission and mandate to teach life-giving principles from God's Word in a real, relevant, and practical way that will minister salvation and direction to the lost, healing to the wounded, hope to the broken-hearted, and proclaim freedom to those bound by addictions and imprisoned by despair.

We are honored to have had the opportunity to share our heart with you throughout this resource and now we would love to hear from you! Please visit us at www.JenniferBeckham.org today to:

- Find out how you can make Jesus the Savior and Lord of your life.
- Send us your prayer requests or testimony of God's blessings.
- Become a "GAP" Partner with JBM!
- Access Jennifer's speaking schedule to find out when Jennifer will be in your area—she'd love to meet you!
- Check out her latest blog, podcast, and television appearances.
- Invite Jennifer to speak at your next event.
- Find out about upcoming books, curriculum, and more.

"GET OVER YOURSELF" CURRICULUM NOW AVAILABLE!

Do you find yourself on a never-ending chase for fulfillment? Feeling as though you're "stuck" in life—stuck in the pain and the shame of the past? Or stuck in the misery and the heartaches of today?

Then roll up your sleeves and allow Jennifer to take you by the hand on the journey of a lifetime—a journey to *Get Over Yourself* and on with your destiny!

In this practical and relevant eleven-session teaching series, author and speaker Jennifer Beckham personally walks you through the pages of her book, *Get Over Yourself,* where she masterfully correlates her early days as a Disney "Princess" with her present life as God's princess to powerfully and effectively teach you—and women of all ages—how to get beyond the pain, the shame and the heartaches of life in order to achieve balance, fulfillment, confidence, and a true purpose for living.

A seamless companion to Jennifer's popular book, each compelling video segment includes author's insights, teaching footage from one of Jennifer's Get Over Yourself conferences, as well as commentary and questions to initiate group discussion, interactions, and practical application.

Read a chapter of the book during the week, then watch the corresponding video and discuss the topic at the group meeting.*

Includes 2 promotional videos and a downloadable poster.

Perfect for church, small group, or individual study.

(11 Sessions on 4 DVD's)

*Books sold separately.

Companion workbook and leader's guide also sold separately.

For more info about this and other available products, please visit: JenniferBeckham.org

DESTINY IMAGE PUBLISHERS, INC.

*"Speaking to the Purposes of God for This Generation
and for the Generations to Come."*

VISIT OUR NEW SITE HOME AT
WWW.DESTINYIMAGE.COM

FREE SUBSCRIPTION TO DI NEWSLETTER

Receive free unpublished articles by top DI authors, exclusive
discounts, and free downloads from our best and newest books.
Visit www.destinyimage.com to subscribe.

Write to: Destiny Image
P.O. Box 310
Shippensburg, PA 17257-0310

Call: 1-800-722-6774

Email: orders@destinyimage.com

For a complete list of our titles or to place an order
online, visit www.destinyimage.com.

FIND US ON **FACEBOOK** OR FOLLOW US ON **TWITTER**.

www.facebook.com/destinyimage   **facebook**
www.twitter.com/destinyimage   **twitter**